2450

# VERYONE'S GUIDE TO HOME COMPOSTING

## ROBYN BEM

VNR VAN NOSTRAND REINHOLD COMPANY
New York  Cincinnati  Toronto  London  Melbourne

Copyright ©1978 by Litton Educational Publishing, Inc.

Library of Congress Catalog Card Number 77-27264
ISBN 0-442-20682-8 (cloth)
ISBN 0-442-20680-1 (paper)

Printed in the United States of America.

Published in 1978 by Van Nostrand Reinhold Company
A division of Litton Educational Publishing, Inc.
135 West 50th Street, New York, NY 10020, U.S.A.

Van Nostrand Reinhold Limited
1410 Birchmount Road
Scarborough, Ontario M1P 2E7, Canada

Van Nostrand Reinhold Australia Pty. Ltd.
17 Queen Street
Mitcham, Victoria 3132, Australia

Van Nostrand Reinhold Company Limited
Molly Millars Lane
Wokingham, Berkshire, England

16   15   14   13   12   11   10   9   8   7   6   5   4   3   2   1

Library of Congress Cataloging in Publication Data

Bem, Robyn.
    Everyone's guide to home composting.

    Bibliography:  p.
    Includes index.
    1. Compost.  I.  Title.
S661.B45                    668'.63'75                    77-27264
ISBN 0-442-20682-8
ISBN 0-442-20680-1 pbk.

# TO PACHAMAMA

*The Andes Mountains*

Much encouragement and assistance was given by many good friends and fellow companions of the earth. Special thanks must go to Gary Chassman for all his help in editing, to Jean Wall Penland for her illustrations, to Karen Wasiolek for her tiny bird and mouse illustrations, and to Jorge Young for allowing us to use his photograph of the Andes Mountains.

# CONTENTS

EASY REFERENCE GUIDE FOR BUILDING
YOUR COMPOST HEAP (TO REMOVE AND
USE AT YOUR WORK AREA)

EASY REFERENCE GUIDE FOR BUILDING
A SIMPLE WOODEN BIN (TO REMOVE AND
USE AT YOUR WORK AREA)

# INTRODUCTION

The earth is teeming with life. Within a handful of soil lies a population of millions and millions of minute organisms which are living, growing, working, and dying. Bacteria, fungi, and earthworms grow and multiply, building their bodies from the nutrients in the soil. They work and help provide plants with the nutrients they need to grow. In time, the soil organisms die and decay, releasing additional nutrients the plants can use. The plants grow and feed us. We usually use only a part of the plant, eating leaves, stems, roots, or fruits. The rest of the plant dies and decays with the help of the soil organisms. The simple nutrients of life are recycled. The earth is the source of our being.

The life within the soil needs to be nourished if it is to survive. The source of nourishment is *organic matter*, materials which once were living, such as leaves from trees and manure from animals. Organic matter enriches the soil. The soil organisms thrive and contribute to the healthy growth of the plants from which we derive our well-being.

In every forest, grassland, or jungle you can see the way in which nature recycles all the organic materials deposited by plants and animals. In the forest, looking underneath the leaves that have fallen to the ground you can see layers of accumulated materials. The changing of seasons brings the addition of twigs and leaves to the forest floor. Birds drop feathers and scatter seeds they have gathered. Flowers and grasses live their cycle of the season flowering, fruiting, and letting go their seed. Forest animals forage for food, passing seeds and other substances their bodies cannot utilize. These materials accumulate in layers on the forest floor. The organic materials in the layers progressively break down (decompose). Several layers beneath the forest floor, the leaves become difficult to distinguish. Here you are looking at a rich, loose layer of leaf "compost." With warmth and moisture, the bacteria, fungi, and earthworms have worked to convert the "complex" structure of the leaves to compost. Compost provides the nutrients and organic matter for fertile soil. Forest life is continually nourished by this reservoir of food and energy.

Just as nature recycles its organic materials, we can combine many of the materials commonly considered as "waste" and help change them to compost, a form which readily nourishes the earth. Plants need healthy soil. Plants grown in healthy soil contain plentiful amounts of vitamins and minerals. The vitamins and minerals which they absorb from the soil are passed on to us. The health of the plants we grow for ourselves and our families directly affects our personal health and well-being.

Bearwallow Mountain
Summer, 1977

# 1. HOW COMPOST NOURISHES THE EARTH, THE PLANTS, AND US

*Compost is a fine soil conditioner.* Compost plays a vital role in making the physical environment of soils suitable for the growth of healthy crops. With the help of microorganisms, the particles of the soil are grouped and held together, furnishing the soil with a good structure. This increases the capacity of the soil to absorb and retain water. (Compost holds 9 times its weight of water, which is 900 percent retention, compared to sand which holds less than 2 percent, and clay which retains 20 percent.[1] Peat moss absorbs approximately 15 times its weight of water, although it contains few, if any, nutrients.) Good soil structure allows plant roots to develop and penetrate the soil extensively, providing resistance against erosion by water and wind. Soil to which compost has been added is considerably easier to work.

The importance of good soil structure is that it facilitates circulation of water and air. A heavy clay soil which has poor structure tends to become waterlogged or to slick over on the surface, preventing water and air penetration. The addition of compost helps to loosen up clay soil by opening up pore spaces. A "crumb" structure is built, and a thin film of moisture is held on each crumb of soil where plant roots can utilize it as needed. Sandy soil, which tends to allow water to drain away rapidly, is also given a "crumb" structure with the addition of organic matter.[2]

*Compost provides a continuous balance of nutrients.* Compost can be a source of nearly all the known elements needed by plants. These include the major plant foods of nitrogen (N), phosphorus (P), and potassium (K), as well as calcium, magnesium, iron, copper, and zinc. Although some of these (and others not mentioned) are needed only in very small amounts, all are important to the strong, healthy growth of plants and animals.

Plants grow well in soil to which compost has been added. Compost is lower in nitrogen, phosphorus, and potassium compared to commercial NPK fertilizers. A higher percentage of NPK on a bag of fertilizer is not an indication that the plants will grow better in soil that contains that particular fertilizer. A healthy soil contains much more than just nitrogen, phosphorus, and potassium.

Unlike commercial fertilizers, compost releases a constant supply of available nitrogen. As the organic matter in the compost continues to decompose, small amounts of nitrogen (and other nutrients) are released. A *gradual* supply of nitrogen is very important. When there is too much or too little nitrogen in the soil, crop productivity declines. The nitrogen in commercial fertilizer dissolves easily in water and can be leached from the soil during heavy rains. When commercial fertilizer is applied in large quantities, it provides an overload of available nitrogen. An excessive amount of nitrogen produces weak plants: The cells of the plant leaves grow larger, have thinner walls, and contain proportionately more water. Many insects are attracted to just this kind of plant growth and will remind you of the state of your soil as they munch heartily on your weakened crops.

*Compost influences the availability of nutrients in several other ways.* Plant nutrients, which may otherwise be lost through leaching, are held in a readily available form for growing plants by sticky substances—*colloids*—found in organic matter. These same substances help create the water-holding capacity that prevents erosion.

Compost also helps make minerals that are already present in the soil (like iron, copper, zinc, and manganese) available to the plants. It does this through the presence of substances called *chelators*, which grasp and hold on to minerals which were previously unavailable to the plants.

# 2. A PLACE TO COMPOST

Wherever you live, it is possible for you to find a suitable place to compost nearly all your household and garden "waste." As you look around for a place, keep in mind that it is important to find a good home for the organisms which do all the work of decomposing the organic materials for you.

Several important ideas may help you to decide on the location for the compost heap: It is helpful to have enough space for a wheelbarrow or wagon in order to easily move materials to the heap and the resulting compost to the garden. A nearby water supply is needed at times to maintain the moisture in the heap, in case there is not enough rainfall. A place sheltered somewhat from the sun, wind, and excessive rain will help prevent the compost from becoming too dry or waterlogged, allowing it to stay warm and moist.

Trees or shrubs provide some protection from sun, wind, and rain. Alder, hazelnut, birch, elderberry, and oak are a few types of trees under which it is good to build your compost heap. The compost heap should be a distance of at least 3 feet from the tree trunk, so as not to provide a shelter for insects which may be harmful to the tree.

Some types of trees or shrubs may not offer good shelter. Various substances contained in the leaves and other litter which fall from the trees into the compost heap may have an adverse effect. Plants to avoid are poisonous plants (oleander), plants whose leaves decompose slowly (magnolia), plants whose acids are toxic to other plants (eucalyptus), or those which contain substances that may interfere with decomposition, such as pine needles, which are very acid and contain a form of kerosene.[1]

# 3. COMPOST BINS, HEAPS, AND PITS

Composting methods vary. Your circumstances will determine how you choose to compost. If you live in the city or its suburbs, you can compost in a bin or pit. A compost bin will neatly contain your compost in a small space. If you live on a farm or have a large space in which to garden, a large open compost heap is more practical. On a farm, it is likely that you will continually recycle more materials than a small compost bin can easily handle. If you live in an area with excessive rainfall or cold winds, try building several large compost bins or compost in a pit or long trench. Try different ways of composting to determine which is more to your liking.

## COMPOST BINS

Small-scale composting often requires the use of a bin. Small compost heaps do not retain heat well. The temperature of a compost heap is most affected by the cooling, drying effect of wind. A compost heap needs to have dimensions of at least 3 feet by 3 feet by 3 feet (1 cubic yard) in order to be sufficiently self-insulating to retain its heat. In colder climates, a larger volume may be needed for sufficient insulation. A compost bin alleviates problems of insulation for small heaps or heaps that are accumulated gradually. A bin also helps to protect the compost heap from scavenging animals.

Bins can be built in many different ways. Try building your bin from secondhand materials. It is best to leave spaces in the walls of the bin in order to allow air to penetrate the heap. Leave 1/2- to 1 1/2-inch spaces between wooden slats, depending on their width. Concrete blocks or bricks, stones, straw bales, barrels, boxes, or wire fencing can also be used.

A wooden bin provides a sturdy container for a compost heap. Instructions on how to build a simple wooden compost bin are given in this chapter.

A double wooden bin with a removable middle wall provides an easy way to turn the compost heap.

A series of bins can be built to accommodate more than one compost heap. This would allow you to build a new compost heap while another is "ripening." The top bin is filled first, and when the material is ready for turning, it is dropped into the bins below. (Reprinted from *The Complete Book of Composting* © 1960 by J. I. Rodale. Permission granted by Rodale Press, Inc., Emmaus, Pa. 18049, p. 221).

A picket fence bin is easy to assemble. The sections of fencing can be fastened in 2 angled sections and hooked together. When the compost heap is ready to be turned, you simply unhook the sections of the bin and reassemble it next to the original compost heap.

A cylinder of wire fencing, the ends of which are fastened together with chain snaps, makes a simple compost bin. (Reprinted from *The Complete Book of Composting* © 1960 by J. I. Rodale. Permission granted by Rodale Press, Inc., Emmaus, Pa. 18049, p. 213).

A wire bin can be insulated by surrounding it with leaves and straw. A piece of burlap helps to protect the top of the bin from rain and snow, enabling you to make compost during the winter months. (Reprinted from *The Complete Book of Composting* © 1960 by J. I. Rodale. Permission granted by Rodale Press, Inc., Emmaus, Pa. 18049, p. 216).

A wooden bin with finished dimensions of 3 by 3 by 3 feet can be constructed with readily available materials.

## BUILDING A SIMPLE WOODEN BIN

*Materials*

Wood
  Frame: 2 pieces, 2 by 2 by 36 inches
         2 pieces, 2 by 2 by 38 inches
  Sides: 32 pieces, 1 by 4 by 36 inches
  Furring strips: 2 pieces, 1 by 3 by 36 inches
  Roof: 1 piece, 40-inch square
        (or half an old door)
        (or corrugated tin)
  *Caution:* Actual wood sizes are smaller than the dimensions given. When you ask for a 1- by 4-inch piece of wood, the actual size is 3/4 by 3 1/2 inches.
Hardware
  # 3 galvanized nails (1 1/4-inch)
  # 6 galvanized nails (2-inch)
  4 medium-sized hasps (2 1/2-inch)

*Instructions*

1. Place the 38-inch frame posts toward the front side of the bin, and the 36-inch frame posts toward the rear.
2. Nail the side slats to the frame posts, leaving 1-inch spaces between slats. (The front frame posts must be 3/4 inch from the end of the slats to allow sufficient space for the furring strips which hold the front gate together. The front gate must lie flat against the rest of the frame.)
3. Nail the rear slats to the 36-inch frame posts to complete 3 sides of the bin.

4. Nail the front slats to the furring strips and attach the 4 hasps to hold the front gate to the frame.
5. Set the roof over the bin frame. The roof slants toward the rear of the bin to direct heavy rain run-off. The roof can be removed and replaced to regulate watering, catching rainfall as needed.

*Note:* If you want to treat the wood of your bin to preserve it longer, use linseed oil. Creosote should not be used on compost bins, because it is a toxic substance which can hinder the growth of microorganisms and plants.

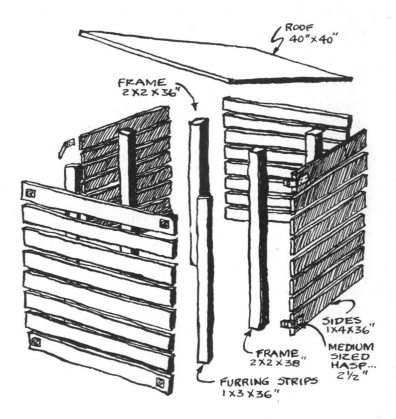

ROOF
40"x40"

FRAME
2x2x36"

SIDES
1x4x36"

FRAME
2x2x38"

MEDIUM
SIZED
HASP...
2½"

FURRING STRIPS
1x3x36"

## OPEN COMPOST HEAPS

Larger compost heaps can be made without an enclosure. It is preferable to build an open compost heap all at once, rather than accumulating small amounts of materials over a long period of time. If your supply of compost materials is limited, build a smaller heap. When you have accumulated more materials, build another complete heap. The first one can be used while the second one is "ripening." A compost heap which is built gradually contains layers of materials which are in different stages of decomposition. The finished compost is on the bottom of the heap, not easily accessible for use until the rest of the heap is fully decomposed. In autumn and spring, composting materials are abundant, making it easy to build a large compost heap in a very short time.

Good insulation of an open compost heap is important, especially if your area has frequent, heavy rains or particularly cold winters. A layer of soil and a thick covering of hay is generally used for insulation. Burlap material can provide additional insulation. Plastic is not a good material to use because it does not allow the circulation of air.

Large-scale composting, as is done commercially, usually involves the use of windrows. A windrow is a long compost heap, perhaps 8 to 10 feet wide at the base. Tractor plows are used extensively to turn windrows. A large machine has been developed which straddles the heap, turning it as it passes over. Commercial windrows are turned often to increase the rate of decomposition.

Windrows may also be used on a smaller scale, allowing for new materials to be added at one end, while finished compost is removed from the other.  If necessary, turning can be done by hand or with the help of a small garden plow.

## COMPOST PITS

Compost can be made in pits, or trenches. This method results in better insulation, but poor air circulation. A compost pit may be of any convenient width or length. The depth of the pit should be 1 foot or more, depending on the volume of materials you are going to compost and your inclination for digging. The excavated soil is generally used in the building of the compost heap and can also be used to form a lip or wall at ground level. Fill the pit slightly over ground level, since the original materials will lose some volume as they decompose. Cover the pit with wooden planks so that no one steps into it accidentally. Once the pit is filled, cover the materials with a layer of soil to reduce odor and prevent flies from laying eggs on the compost materials. A covering layer of straw will help to insulate the materials and lessen the evaporation of moisture which normally occurs.

The finished compost in the pit can be used as a planting bed or moved to another location. Root crops, like carrots or beets, grow well in compost beds. Be sure to plant only when the compost materials have thoroughly decomposed or the plants will suffer from nitrogen hunger. The bacteria decomposing the compost materials compete for the nitrogen. The healthy growth of the plants is inhibited if not enough nitrogen is available for both the plants and the bacteria.

# 4. GATHERING THE MATERIALS

Compost materials are plentiful. Many materials which can be composted are continually discarded by households, restaurants, groceries, communities, and industries. All that you need to gather an abundance of materials to compost is energy—your own and perhaps fuel for a vehicle. Strong boxes to contain compost materials can be found at book stores, liquor stores, and groceries. I would suggest gathering a large amount and variety of compost materials at one time, so that it requires little effort to combine many different materials in the compost heap each time you add to it or start another heap.

A variety of materials from different sources provides a variety and balance of nutrients in the compost. The materials described here are only a few of those easily found in any community. The materials listed first are likely to be found in your home and garden or within a short distance. Several lists of compost materials and their percentage content of nitrogen, phosphoric acid (available form of phosphorus), and potash (available form of potassium) are found in Appendix I.

## KITCHEN, GROCERY, AND RESTAURANT WASTE

The various vegetable and fruit trimmings available in households, groceries, and restaurants are rich in nitrogen and other nutrients, including trace elements.  If you decide to build your compost heap gradually, kitchen waste can be put in a tight-lidded container until enough has been accumulated for a layer.  Sawdust placed in the bottom of the container absorbs the juices of the garbage.  An occasional sprinkling of limestone or wood ash helps prevent odor, discourages flies from laying their eggs, and neutralizes the acidity of the raw garbage.  Manure or rich soil can be added to give the kitchen garbage a good start on composting.

A layer of kitchen waste in the compost heap is covered with a layer of manure and a thin layer of rich soil.  Manure and rich soil contribute microorganisms and nutrients and also prevent flies from laying eggs on the garbage.  A properly built compost heap does not give off strong odors and does not attract rodents or flies . . . or outraged neighbors.

*Banana skins* are rich in potassium and phosphorus.  The skins readily decompose, indicating a high nitrogen content.

*Bones* are a good source of phosphorus, as well as nitrogen.  When bones are steamed (in a pressure cooker) or boiled until soft, their fatty materials are removed and they can be ground more easily, hastening their decay.  Bone meal helps to reduce acidity in the compost heap because of its lime content.

*Citrus rinds* are easily composted. If the rinds are thick, they tend to be richer in nitrogen. Orange, lemon, and grapefruit rinds contain varying amounts of phosphorus and potassium. You can encourage decomposition if you chop up the rinds somewhat before adding them to the compost heap.

*Coffee grounds* contain nitrogen and small amounts of phosphorus and potassium. Coffee grounds preserve moisture well and, because of this, they sour easily. Mixed with ground limestone, the grounds are a good addition to the compost. They have been shown to contain many minerals, including trace elements, plus carbohydrates (sugars) and some vitamins.

*Corn cobs* are fairly resistant to decomposition, but, cut up or ground, they are a good material for compost. The cob, in nutrient value, is said to be 2/3 that of the kernel. Corn cobs can be combined with leaves to prevent the leaves from matting and hindering aeration of the compost heap.

*Eggshells* consist mainly of calcium. The shells provide lime, thus helping to reduce acidity in the compost heap. Crushing the shells aids in their decomposition.

*Grease* (including oily salad scraps): DO NOT USE. Grease decomposes slowly. Grease can coat other materials in the compost heap, hindering their decomposition.

*Nutshells* such as walnut, almond, and pecan may resist breaking down. These can best be used in a special compost heap made of hard-to-decompose materials or as a mulch. Peanut shells break down easily and are a good source of nitrogen for the compost heap.

*Tea leaves* are good to use in the compost heap. The leaves add various minerals, nitrogen, and small amounts of phosphorus and potassium. Tea leaves contained in a filter bag can be added as is. The filter paper will decompose with the other compost materials.

## HAIR

Hair and feathers are high in nitrogen content.  Hair is easily gathered at barber or hair-styling shops.  To prevent matting, the hair should be cut in short pieces and combined with other materials.

## LEAVES

Leaves contain many minerals absorbed and brought up from deep soil by the tree roots.  Many of the nutrients which have leached out of the surface layer of the soil are replenished when the leaves fall and decompose.  Leaves are made up of large amounts of fibrous organic matter, giving them a good soil-building quality.  It is best to chop and mix green leaves with other materials as they tend to obstruct air circulation in the compost heap by matting.  Dry leaves can be crushed.

Not all leaves are good to use in the compost heap. Eucalyptus, California bay, walnut, juniper, camphor, acacia, cypress, and pittosporum either decompose too slowly to be mixed with other materials or contain resins or acids which can impede the growth of microorganisms and plants.[1] Walnut leaves contain juglanic acid, which is toxic, and hinders the growth of such plants as apple trees and tomatoes.[2] Some leaves can be used abundantly in a compost heap, as long as a good source of nitrogen is provided. Oak leaf compost is good material for acid-loving plants, such as tomatoes or blueberries.

## GRASS CLIPPINGS

Grass clippings are a good, abundant material containing nitrogen. When a pile of freshly cut grass is left undisturbed for several days, you will find that it becomes very hot in the center. The heat generated by the pile of grass clippings is an indication that it is decomposing. When green grass is not mixed with a drier, absorbent material, it tends to compact and prevent air circulation. The moisture contained in the grass may transform the pile into a wet, brown mess. When using grass in the compost heap, it is important to mix green grass clippings with a coarser material such as dry leaves or wood shavings. Alternatively, you can dry the grass before adding it to the compost heap.

It is important to choose your source of grass clippings carefully. Avoid grass which is growing along busy streets. Roadside vegetation accumulates lead from continuous exposure to car exhaust. Do not use grass which has been sprayed for dandelions or other unwanted growth. Grass clippings are so abundant that there is no need to ever consider using any that are of questionable quality.

## WEEDS

Weeds and garden debris are good compost materials. Many plants accumulate particular minerals, such as dandelion which accumulates calcium. Minerals which have been accumulated in weeds can be returned to the soil through composting.

Weeds such as Bermuda grass, couch grass, and bindweed should be thoroughly dried in the sun before being added to the compost heap. Green succulent material should be withered so that it decomposes, rather than continuing to grow in the heap. Thick stalks of cabbage, corn, and other garden vegetables should be chopped into short lengths and crushed to break up some of the tough fibers.

Weed seeds are not a problem if the compost heap is built correctly. The heat produced in the heap is sufficient to make the seeds inviable. Of course, the easiest solution is to "harvest" the weeds before they flower and go to seed.

## SOIL

Soil is generally used in compost heaps. Fertile soil contributes a large population of organisms which help decompose the compost materials, as well as minerals which the organisms need to live. Soil also helps prevent the loss of nitrogen to the air in the form of ammonia gas. Use very thin layers of soil—perhaps 1/8 inch—in the compost heap. It is important not to use too much soil, because it may add too much weight to the heap and compress the materials underneath. Soil is used as an insulating layer after the compost heap is completed. A 2-inch cover layer is sufficient to conserve moisture and heat.

Previously made compost is an alternative to soil, contributing both organisms and minerals. Using compost as an ingredient in a new compost heap is similar in effect to using yogurt as a starter when making a new batch of yogurt. The compost starter contributes the necessary organisms for decomposing the new compost materials.

## MANURE

Manure can be used generously in the compost heap. Manure supplies nitrogen and a large population of bacteria. If some kind of straw or sawdust litter is used as bedding for the animals, urine is absorbed and nearly all the nutrients voided by the animals are preserved. Manure which is stored in piles without being mixed with straw or sawdust litter generally loses a large proportion of its nitrogen, either to the air in the form of ammonia gas or through leaching by rainfall. Composted manure is a much better source of nitrogen, since the nitrogen is held by the active microorganisms. It is good to use manure from different animals, including that of dogs, cats, rabbits, and birds. The different manures contribute a variety of nutrients and organisms to the compost heap. Manure can be gathered from riding stables and beef or poultry farms. Generally, the manure is free and its removal is appreciated by the stable keeper or farmer.

## STRAW

Straw and hay supply much carbon material (energy food for the bacteria) and bulk to the compost heap, as well as various nutrients. If straw is used in large quantities, it is good to chop it up and mix it with other materials which hold water and contain a rich source of nitrogen. Manure helps to hold moisture on the smooth, hard surfaces of strawy materials. Generally, straw and hay are not thought to contain nitrogen, but alfalfa hay is known as a fairly rich source of it. Straw or hay can be found at riding stables or farms. Hay which has been exposed to rain is considered "spoiled," since it then cannot be fed to the animals. Often you can gather "spoiled" hay for free, simply by making the effort to cart it away.

## SAWDUST

Sawdust and wood shavings are helpful in absorbing excess moisture in the compost heap. Woody materials contain lignin, or wood fiber, which gives strength and hardness to the cells of wood. These materials decompose slowly and need to be combined with manure or another nitrogen source. Sawdust and wood shavings contribute much organic matter. When added in thin layers or mixed with other materials, sawdust and wood shavings help give the compost heap structural strength. It is easy to find free sawdust and wood shavings at lumberyards, cabinet shops, or sawmills.

## WOOD ASH

Wood ash is a valuable source of potassium. Save the wood ash from your fireplace or wood stove and store it carefully. It should not be exposed to rainfall, as the potassium is rather easily leached out. Wood ash may replace limestone as an acid neutralizer in the compost heap. Do not use coal ash in the compost heap. Coal ash can add toxic quantities of sulfur and iron.

## LIMESTONE

Limestone has a neutralizing effect on the materials used in a compost heap and provides a source of calcium and small amounts of minerals. Ground limestone breaks down gradually, releasing available nutrients over a long period of time. Dolomite, a rock similar to limestone, is interchangeable with it. It is possible to add too much limestone to a compost heap. The result can be an increased loss of nitrogen to the air in the form of ammonia gas. I have not experienced this in the compost heaps I have built, so I continue to sprinkle a *light* layer of limestone over each layer of kitchen garbage or mix it with each soil layer.

Do not substitute quicklime for ground limestone. When sufficient water is not available, the quicklime wrenches water from bacteria, fungi, and plant roots, usually causing their death.[3] Quicklime also increases nitrogen loss by causing the formation of ammonia. Slaked lime (hydrate of lime) is not a good substitute either. Unlike ground limestone, which is gradually available, slaked lime is in a readily available form. Slaked lime dissolves easily in water and leaches down to soil levels where it cannot be reached by plant roots.[4] Wood ash and bone meal can be used instead of limestone.

## PHOSPHATE ROCK

Phosphate rock is a good source of phosphorus for the compost heap. It also contains minerals such as iron, copper, zinc, and magnesium. If you have tested your soil and found that it is rather low in phosphorus, add phosphate rock to the compost heap. When the compost is added to the soil, phosphorus is incorporated in balance with other nutrients. A light sprinkling of phosphate rock in various layers of the compost heap will supply enough phosphorus to maintain a healthy soil. Phosphate rock also helps to preserve nitrogen in the compost heap by combining with ammonia. If your soil is very low in phosphorus, add phosphate rock directly to the soil, as well as adding it to the compost heap. Phosphate rock can be found at nurseries and garden-supply stores.

Phosphate rock is made available to plants gradually as it is needed. It remains in the soil until plant roots grow in the surrounding area. The plant roots give off carbon dioxide ($CO_2$) and acids which help dissolve the phosphate rock, releasing its nutrients. The microorganisms help to combine the minerals of the phosphate rock into compounds which plants absorb easily.

Superphosphate is not a substitute for phosphate rock. Many of the minerals found in phosphate rock are inactivated when superphosphate is processed. Superphosphate is treated with sulfuric acid to make it more soluble and can create an imbalance in the population of microorganisms living in the compost heap and the soil. The bacteria that break down the sulfur multiply and feed on particular fungi which help to break down cellulose.[5] A large proportion of plant tissue is made of cellulose. Superphosphate would, therefore, slow down the decomposition of such compost materials as hay, leaves, and sawdust.

## COTTONSEED MEAL

Cottonseed meal is made from the cottonseed which has had its lints, hulls, and its oil removed. Cottonseed meal is primarily used as a good source of nitrogen, but also contains phosphorus, potassium, and trace elements. The meal, easy and pleasant to handle, is acidic and is a good material to use in making compost for acid-loving plants.

## SEAWEED

Easily found on or near shore, seaweed is a good material to add to a compost heap. Seaweed should be quickly rinsed to remove excess salt and used in the compost heap immediately. Some of the seaweeds generally used are kelp or driftweed (Laminaria), bladder wrack or cutweed (Fucus), and sea lettuce (Ulva). Seaweed contains some nitrogen and is a particularly rich source of potassium, minerals, and vitamins. The main structural material of seaweed is alginic acid. Alginic acid can act as a colloid in the compost heap, combining with minerals and holding moisture, helping to prevent the loss of nutrients through leaching. Seaweed, combined with manure or another nitrogen source, makes a good mixture that aids in the rapid decay of straw or similar compost materials.

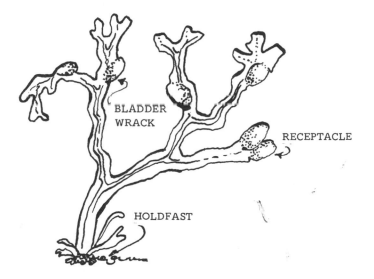

Bladder Wrack or Cutweed (Fucus)

# 5. CHOPPING AND SHREDDING

Chopping and shredding increase the surface area of the compost materials. The smaller the size of the materials, the more surface area exposed to the bacteria and other compost organisms. Compost materials decompose more rapidly when they are chopped or shredded. Chopping and shredding of the materials results in better insulation, less loss of heat and moisture, and improved aeration throughout the heap (there is less of a tendency for the materials to mat or pack down). Turning is easier and the finished compost is more uniform.

## TOOLS AND EQUIPMENT

A *machete*, a *cleaver*, or a *sharp spade* is the simplest (and least expensive) tool to use for chopping compost materials. Chop up stalks of corn and cabbage and crush them to expose more surface area. Cut up tomato vines and stems of garden vegetables like beans and peppers. Chop up green leaves or let them dry and then crush them. Crush eggshells and cut up kitchen scraps into small pieces while you are preparing vegetables and fruits.

A *wire mesh leaf shredder* can be built from a wooden box. Replace the bottom with 1/2-inch wire mesh. Add 2 pieces of wood on the bottom to act as legs to provide clearance for the finished material to fall through.[1]

A *reel (hand) lawn mower* can be converted into a shredder. Remove the handle and braces of the mower. Mount the mower so that the cutting bar is in a vertical position and is flush with the bottom of the feeding trough of the wooden table. The feeding trough should have sides 3 or 4 inches high and a bottom which will permit easy feeding of the plant material into the machine. The trough can be lined with galvanized metal. Drill a small hole halfway between the center and edge of one wheel and attach a handle with a bolt and nut. The machine can be operated by hand, as shown in the drawing, or with a motor mounted on a platform attached to a leg or frame of the machine. The pulley attached to the motor should be relatively small, while that on the lawn mower wheel should be much larger, so that the machine is not turned too rapidly and does not choke up easily. For feeding the plant material into the machine, use a rectangular piece of board with a handle attached to one side as a pusher.[2]

Reprinted from *The Complete Book of Composting* © 1960 by J. I. Rodale. Permission granted by Rodale Press, Inc., Emmaus, Pa. 18049, p. 239.

A *rotary lawn mower* can be used to shred compost materials. The materials to be shredded are piled on the ground near a wall or fence, and the mower is moved over them several times. If you already own a rotary lawn mower, use it for shredding your compost materials. If you don't have a rotary lawn mower, don't worry about buying one. Chopping your compost materials by hand is sufficient to make good compost.

A *commercial power shredder* can be used, although they are expensive to buy and not necessary for making good compost. The noise generated and the fuel consumed by power shredders makes their value in home composting rather doubtful. Power shredders are helpful in shredding materials for use in mulching. The most efficient use of power shredders is on a neighborhood or community level.

# 6. A GOOD HOME FOR THE COMPOSTERS

The compost heap must be able to support the growth and activity of the compost organisms if it is to work well. Composting is influenced by moisture, temperature, pH (acidity or alkalinity), nutrients, and the amount of oxygen available. If any one of these conditions is unbalanced, the whole composting process is affected. As you build the compost heap and take care of it, you need to think about the composters and be watchful for indications that they are not thriving.

## OXYGEN

Composting can be done with or without oxygen. Aerobic composting is done with oxygen. In nature, decomposition is most commonly aerobic. On the forest floor, droppings from trees and animals are converted to compost through aerobic decomposition.

*Aerobic composting* involves high temperatures. High temperatures are important to inactivate weed seeds, insect eggs, and harmful microorganisms which may be present. An aerobic compost heap does not give off unpleasant odors. The organisms involved work rapidly. For these reasons, I feel aerobic composting is best for home composters.

An aerobic compost heap needs to be able to breathe. Build your compost heap loosely. Sufficient air space needs to be left to allow a flow of oxygen throughout the heap and the escape of carbon dioxide. Materials like sawdust and coffee grounds have a texture which tends to compact when moist. If you mix these materials with more fibrous, bulky materials, such as leaves, they will be less likely to prevent aeration of the compost heap.

Your nose is a good monitor of the oxygen supply in your compost heap. If the heap begins to smell (like rotten eggs), there is not enough oxygen. Turning the heap is the best way to aerate it. (See Chapter 9.) Turning the compost heap helps to eliminate airless patches, which commonly develop even in a compost heap which has been carefully built.

*Anaerobic composting* is done without oxygen. Anaerobic composting is often considered to be an easier way to compost, since little attention is needed to maintain the conditions. A simple way to compost without oxygen is to build a compost heap and cover it with heavy plastic, holding the edges down with soil or rocks. The following season you can add the compost to your garden soil. Another method is to enclose the compost materials in a plastic bag. The bag should be turned over often to expose all sides to the warmth of the sun.

Anaerobic composting has its disadvantages. The organisms in an anaerobic compost heap work slowly. This may not concern you if you have plenty of composting space and are not using a large amount of compost in your garden regularly. A real potential source of discomfort with anaerobic composting is that it produces disagreeable odors. The odors may not be noticed if the compost heap is contained well, although some unpleasantness may be experienced when you uncover the compost to add it to your soil. Compost made by anaerobic methods needs to be added to well-aerated soil. The anaerobic organisms do not do a complete job of decomposing compost materials. Well-aerated soil supports the growth of beneficial organisms which will convert the compost nutrients to forms easily used by the plants.

An important reason many people compost under airless conditions is to reduce the loss of nitrogen to the atmosphere. Manure stored efficiently in an open pit can lose as much as 40 percent of its original nitrogen to the atmosphere. Manure stored in a closed, airless pit loses 5 to 10 percent of its nitrogen.[1]   In addition to preserving nitrogen, anaerobic composting of manure produces a source of fuel—methane. With the use of a special digester tank, methane gas can be recovered as a fuel for cooking, heating, and refrigeration.

## MOISTURE

The compost heap needs to be moist for the compost organisms to thrive. The moistness of the heap should be similar to a damp sponge or towel which has been wrung out. If the compost heap is too dry, the compost organisms cannot work. If the compost heap is too wet, anaerobic conditions develop and an unpleasant odor results. A soggy condition can be changed by turning the compost heap and adding some absorbent material, such as sawdust.

The best way to moisten the compost heap initially is to water the layers as you add them. The amount of water needed depends on the materials. Green grass and kitchen garbage contain enough moisture of their own. Dry leaves, sawdust, and straw need to be watered. A fine spray of water is less apt to disturb the structure of the heap than is a forceful spray. You should moisten the materials thoroughly, but not so much that excess water flows from the bottom of the pile. Many nutrients will be lost from the compost heap if it is saturated in this way.

Check your compost heap for moisture often. Reach into the center of the heap with your hands. The materials should feel warm and moist. If you notice ants in the compost heap, it is too dry and needs to be watered. Be sure that the water penetrates the heap, not just the outer surface layers. Conditions in the compost heap need to be consistent throughout for even decomposition.

## PH:  ACID TO ALKALINE

Years ago farmers used to taste their soil to determine how well crops would grow in it.  If the soil tasted sour or bitter, the farmer knew that crops would not grow well. Sweet-tasting soil was a good indication that crops would thrive.

People now use several other ways to find out if their soil is acid or alkaline.  A simple test can be done with litmus paper, available at most drugstores.  Litmus paper is placed in direct contact with moist soil or compost.  If the soil is alkaline, the paper turns blue.  If the soil is acid, the paper turns pink.  No color change occurs when the soil is neutral. Another kind of test paper is available through scientific supply companies.  The paper comes in ribbon form, along with a color chart.  A piece of the paper ribbon is dipped into a solution made of distilled water and a sample of your soil or compost.  The colors appearing on the paper are then compared to the color chart to determine the degree of acidity or alkalinity.

Chemical tests are widely used to test for pH.  You can either send a soil sample to your State or County Agricultural Extension Service, to a private soil-testing laboratory, or you can test it yourself with a simple soil-testing kit.  Easy directions are provided for preparing the test mixture.  The color of the resulting solution is compared with a color chart.  The results are translated to a pH scale of 0 to 14.  The term pH

is a chemical abbreviation used to indicate acidity or alkalinity. A pH of 7.0 is neutral; a pH reading of less than 7.0 is acid; over 7.0 is alkaline.

Most common plants will grow well in soil which is slightly acid-to-neutral, with a pH of 6.5 to 7.0. Soils with plenty of organic matter will support healthy plant growth even if the pH is low or high. Organic matter acts as a pH buffer.

The compost heap provides a good environment for bacteria and fungi when its pH is between 6 and 7.5. Too little oxygen and an excessive amount of moisture can cause the compost heap to become too acid for the bacteria and fungi to work and multiply. An acid condition can be adjusted by turning and aerating the heap, adding some absorbent material, and sprinkling ground limestone or wood ashes over various layers as the heap is rebuilt.

If you test your compost heap for pH during its first week of decomposition, do not be alarmed if you find that it is quite acid. Decaying materials initially tend to be acidic. As the materials decompose, the pH of the compost heap will stabilize and become more neutral.

I use limestone and wood ash in my compost heaps. I feel that they help balance the acid materials that I add to the compost heap, like sawdust and oak leaves. Kitchen garbage is also acidic. A sprinkling of limestone or wood ash over a layer of kitchen garbage helps prevent odor and deters flies from laying eggs.

A low pH affects the availability of nutrients.  Limestone can help make some nutrients available if your compost heap or soil is too acid.  Limestone conditions the compost or soil, helping the soil particles to aggregate, or group together.  Clay soil becomes loose and aerated.  The water retention of sandy soil increases through the use of limestone.  Ground limestone adds calcium to the compost heap.  Dolomitic limestone also adds magnesium.  Wood ashes contribute potassium and phosphorus.

Limestone is alkaline and raises the pH of the compost or soil to which it is added.  The addition of too much limestone can create problems in a compost heap:  The compost organisms cannot work well if their environment is too alkaline.  A high pH affects the availability of some nutrients and may cause others to become toxic.  The loss of nitrogen to the atmosphere in the form of ammonia is increased due to a high pH.  *Light* sprinklings of limestone are sufficient to balance the pH of the compost heap.

## The pH Scale

| Soil pH Conditions and Plant Environment | pH | Verbal Designations of Soil Acidity/ Alkalinity | Familiar Products With Acidity/ Alkalinity Indicated |
|---|---|---|---|
| | 0 | | |
| | 1 | | Hydrochloric acid |
| | | | Phorphoric acid |
| | 2 | | Lemons |
| | | | Vinegar Grapefruit Apples |
| | 3 | | Good grass silage Superphosphate Tomatoes Beer |
| Found rarely in organic soil surface layers | | | |
| Found occasionally in some soils in humid regions | 4 | | |
| Suitable for blueberries, azaleas, and rhododendrons | | Very strongly acid | Poor grass silage |
| Typical of many unlimed soils of humid regions—suitable for potatoes | 5 | Strongly acid | Boric acid Fresh beans |
| Suitable for grasses but 6.5 would be better | | Medium acid | Distilled water open to air |
| Suitable for gardens, commercial vegetables, and grasses | 6 | Slightly acid | Fresh corn |
| Best for growth of most forage crops | | Very slightly acid | Cow's milk |
| Suitable for alfalfa but not necessary; danger of overliming injury on sandy soils | 7 | Neutral, very slightly alkaline | Distilled water in absence of air Human blood |
| Hazard of deficiencies of boron and manganese | | Slightly alkaline | Manure |
| Ground limestone has a pH of 8.3 A pH above 8.3 is caused by sodium | 8 | Medium alkaline | Sea water |
| Found only in alkaline soils of arid West or where materials such as wood ashes have been used in excess | | Strongly alkaline | Bicarbonate of soda |
| | 9 | Very strongly alkaline | |
| | 10 | | Milk of magnesia |
| | 11 | | Ammonia |
| | | | Washing soda |
| | 12 | | Trisodium phosphate |
| | 13 | | Lye |
| | 14 | | |

## TEMPERATURE

The activity of all organisms is very closely related to temperature. Different organisms have different temperature ranges in which they grow and work best. Composting involves temperatures ranging from approximately 15°C (59°F) to 70°C (158°F) and higher. A large or well-insulated compost heap normally reaches high temperatures due to active microorganisms which generate (heat) energy.

When the temperature of a compost heap is above 60°C (140°F), some of the microorganisms become inactive and others die. As protection against destruction by heat, acid conditions, or dryness, some microorganisms enter a spore or resting stage. When conditions are favorable they become active again. The composting process is slower at high temperatures, but high temperatures are important to destroy weed seeds, insect eggs, and harmful organisms which may be present.

Checking the temperature is a good way to monitor the compost heap. You can place a metal rod into the center of the heap and check it occasionally for warmth. Or you can take the temperature of the compost heap with a thermometer. A glass thermometer can be mounted on a stick. A thermometer with a metal probe works well, although it is fairly expensive to buy.

Your compost heap should begin to heat up 1 or 2 days after you build it. The temperature inside the pile (about 12 to 15 inches from the surface) reaches 43°C (110°F) to 49°C (120°F). Within 3 or 4 days, the temperature increases to 54°C (130°F) and higher.[2]   The highest temperature reached may be 75°C (167°F).

The most favorable temperature range for the work of the microorganisms as a whole is 35°C (95°F) to 55°C (131°F).[3]   In this range, many groups of organisms are working actively.   Each group of organisms has a temperature range in which it works best. As the temperature changes, different groups of organisms become active.

The temperature within the compost heap varies. The center of the heap naturally retains the most heat. It is important to expose all the materials to the high heat of the center. In turning the compost heap, you will be moving the outer materials of the heap to the center and the center materials to the outer areas of the heap.

The temperature of the compost heap will remain high until the materials which can readily decompose are stabilized. Then the temperature will drop as the compost organisms become less active. One way to be sure that the compost is ready for use is to turn the heap. The temperature may decline slightly because of the additional air, but will quickly rise again due to the continued activity of the compost organisms. If the temperature does not rise in response to turning and all other conditions in the heap seem favorable for composting, you can be sure that the compost is ready to use. Generally, the temperature at this stage will be under 43°C (110°F).[4]

## NUTRIENTS

Compost materials contain varying amounts of nutrients. The compost organisms need a supply of all the elements their bodies are made of, as well as the elements which give them energy for their work.   A balance of nutrients in the compost heap is important.  If you gather materials from different sources and build your compost heap with various materials, it is likely that you will provide all the nutrients needed by the compost organisms.   The compost added to your soil will supply a balance of nutrients for the plants you grow.

Two nutrients, carbon and nitrogen, are particularly important in building your compost heap.   Materials like straw, sawdust, and leaves contain a high proportion of carbon.   These "dry" materials absorb excess moisture in the compost heap, helping to keep it loose and aerated.  Dry materials also help make the compost heap structurally strong.   Materials like grass clippings and kitchen garbage are generally rich in nitrogen.   These "green" materials contain a large amount of moisture.

The balance of carbon and nitrogen in the compost heap directly affects how well the materials decompose.  Carbon is used by the compost organisms for energy, just as the carbon in carbohydrates is an energy food for us.  Carbon is incorporated into the cells of the compost organisms.

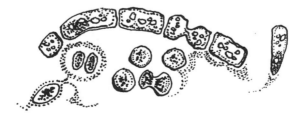

Nitrogen is essential to the growth of the compost organisms. Without nitrogen proteins cannot be synthesized and cells cannot grow. If there is too little nitrogen in the compost heap, the population of organisms is not able to grow and multiply rapidly and decomposition is very slow. This is why a pile of leaves may remain relatively unchanged over a period of a year or two. The growth of the compost organisms is limited by the lack of nitrogen. The microorganisms present in the pile contain nitrogen in their bodies. The nitrogen is recycled as they die and decompose, providing nitrogen for the growth of another population of microorganisms. These organisms work further to decompose the pile of leaves, passing their nitrogen on to the next generation. Gradually, the excess carbon in the pile is used until the leaves are finally decomposed.

How much of which materials should be added to the compost heap? An easy way to combine the materials in a favorable balance is to build the compost heap in layers. The layers vary in size depending on the type of material. A sample series of layers would be: A 5- to 6-inch layer of dry leaves, a 2-inch layer of manure, and a sprinkling (approximately 1/8 inch) of rich topsoil mixed with limestone (or wood ash) and phosphate rock. Chapter 9 contains a more thorough description of how to build your compost heap.

A more technical way to come to understand how to balance carbon and nitrogen in your compost heap is to learn about the Carbon:Nitrogen ratio. If you are not interested in this information, it isn't necessary that you read it. Your experiences in building and taking care of compost heaps will teach you. You will come to know the textures and characteristics of many different materials. You will experience how well your compost heaps decompose or the problems you have with them. Soon you will know how to combine the materials with little effort.

The Carbon:Nitrogen ratio is the term used to describe how much carbon a material contains in relation to nitrogen. Leaves have a C:N ratio of approximately 50:1 (50 to 1). These numbers indicate that leaves contain 50 times as much carbon as nitrogen. Manure is said to have a ratio of 20:1. A lower ratio indicates a higher content of nitrogen. The numbers used in C:N ratios are approximate and tables of C:N should be used only as guides. Tree leaves may have a C:N ratio that varies from 40:1 to 80:1. The nitrogen content of manure may vary greatly depending on the animal source, what the animal is fed, and how the manure is stored.

The most favorable C:N ratio for a compost heap is in the area of 25:1 to 35:1. If you combine similar amounts of leaves (with a ratio of 50:1) and manure (20:1), you will reach a ratio of 35:1.

*Carbon:Nitrogen Ratios of Various Organic Materials*

| | |
|---|---|
| Food wastes (table scraps) | 15:1 |
| Sewage sludge: activated | 6:1 |
| Sewage sludge: digested | 16:1 |
| Wood | 700:1 |
| Sawdust | 500:1 |
| Paper | 170:1 |
| Grass clippings | 19:1 |
| Leaves | a range of 80:1 to 40:1 |
| Fruit wastes | 35:1 |
| Rotted manure | 20:1 |
| Sugar cane residues | 50:1 |
| Cornstalks | 60:1 |
| Straw | 80:1 |
| Alfalfa hay | 12:1 |
| Humus | 10:1 |
| Alfalfa | 13:1 |
| Green sweetclover | 16:1 |
| Mature sweetclover | 23:1 |
| Legume-grass hay | 25:1 |
| Oat straw | 80:1 |

Reprinted from *The Gardener's Guide to Better Soil* © 1975 by Rodale Press, Inc. Permission granted by Rodale Press, Inc., Emmaus, Pa. 18049, p. 150.

# 7. COMPOST ACTIVATORS

A compost activator is any material which stimulates decomposition. Activators introduce microorganisms which break down organic materials and/or contribute nitrogen, providing extra food for the microorganisms. Manure, kitchen garbage, rich soil, and previously made compost are all compost activators.

Special bacterial activators are sold which are said to hasten decomposition and produce a better quality of compost. However, various university studies (University of California, Michigan State University, and Kyoto and Tokyo Universities in Japan) indicate that commercial bacterial activators do not increase the speed or degree of composting. Commercial activators are not essential to making good compost, since microorganisms are already present in the raw materials. Some of the commercial activators sold are high in nitrogen. It is likely that the nitrogen they contribute to the compost heap accounts for their effectiveness.

If you build your compost heap with many different organic materials, there will be sufficient microorganisms in the heap, as well as the nutrients they need to grow. If you make sure that the microorganisms have enough moisture, warmth, and air, they will decompose the materials in your compost heap.

# 8. PREPARING THE SOIL

The compost heap should have free contact with the earth so that the various organisms present in the soil can readily migrate up. If the compost heap is built directly over growing vegetation, particularly grass, an acid layer forms, which acts as a barrier to the entry of earthworms and microorganisms.

A foundation of concrete or a similar material can be used to provide a means of salvaging any liquid run-off from the compost heap. This liquid can then be used to maintain moisture in the pile, preserving some nutrients possibly lost through leaching. Soil must be used in the building of the compost heap to provide bacteria, since the bacteria cannot migrate up into the heap. The heap needs to be turned often to prevent anaerobic conditions from occurring, because the concrete prevents aeration. Overall, it is best to allow free contact of the compost and the soil and to be careful not to overwater the heap.

The composting site needs to be well drained. The ground underneath should be loosened to 1 or 2 feet. I work with a garden spade first, loosening the entire area the compost will rest on. A spading fork can then be used to loosen the soil even more deeply. The dimensions of the composting space depend on how large you choose to make the heap. The area should be at least 3 feet square. A slight slope of the area will help to prevent standing water, which hinders decomposition. When you have finished loosening and raking the area, be careful not to step on and compress the soil you worked so hard to cultivate.

If your soil is sandy, a layer of clay and straw will help provide a foundation for retaining moisture and nutrients in the heap. If you have clay soil, the addition of sand or gravel will improve drainage.

Rich soil, which contains an abundance of organic matter, has a loose and crumbly texture. Many bacteria are naturally found in fertile soil. If your soil does not seem very rich, it would be a good idea to introduce additional bacteria by mixing some manure into the soil before building the compost heap.

# 9. BUILDING AND CARING FOR YOUR COMPOST HEAP

Now that you have decided where you are going to compost and have gathered the compost materials, you can begin to build your compost heap. The compost heap can be left out in the open or enclosed in a bin. The same principles of combining the materials will apply if you have chosen to compost in a pit.

The composting method I will describe to you is one of several possible methods. You may eventually decide to build your compost heaps differently. With a clear understanding of the needs of the compost organisms, you can create your own method of composting.

The guidelines I follow are those developed by Sir Albert Howard. Albert Howard credits the Chinese with the basic ideas, upon which he built his compost heaps.

"It is this return of all wastes to the soil, including the mud of ponds, canals, and ditches, which is the secret of the successful agriculture of the Chinese. The startling thing to realize about this peasant nation of over 400 million souls is the immense period of time over which they have continued to cultivate their fields and keep them fertile, at least 4,000 years."[1]

"The Chinese pay great attention to the making of their compost. Every twig, every dead leaf, every unused stalk is gathered up and every bit of animal excreta and the urine, together with all the wastes of the human population, are incorporated."[2]

Sir Albert Howard believed that healthy soil is basic to the health of plants, animals, and people. Working in Indore, India, in the 1920s, Howard developed a means to maintain soil fertility using the organic materials readily available to the people. The age-old practice of composting provided a source of natural fertilizer for enriching the soil.

Sir Albert Howard, foremost pioneer of organic methods and inventor of the Indore composting system, devoted a lifetime of remote travel and hard work to establishing the scientific principles that support natural agriculture. (Reprinted from *The Complete Book of Composting* © 1960 by J. I. Rodale. Permission granted by Rodale Press, Inc., Emmaus, Pa. 18049, p. 630).

## BUILDING YOUR COMPOST HEAP

### Compost Materials

Branches (an armful or two)
Wooden poles (3 or 4)
Hay
Grass clippings
Leaves
Weeds
Sawdust
Kitchen garbage
Manure (horse, cow,
  chicken, rabbit, dog)
Wood ash or limestone
Rich topsoil
Water

### Getting It All Together

1. Loosen the soil which will be underneath the compost heap. An area at least 3 feet square is a good size to begin with. Add some manure to supply additional bacteria if the soil does not seem fertile.
2. Push 3 or 4 wooden poles into the loosened soil until they stand up easily. Space the poles evenly in the area the compost heap will cover. These will make vertical aeration holes in the compost heap. Other materials which can be used are perforated drainage pipes or cylinders made of chicken wire.
3. Lay down a latticework of branches over the soil. This provides some air circulation underneath the compost heap.
4. Spread a 5- to 6-inch layer of hay, leaves, or other plant materials over the layer of branches. Combine different

materials in each layer. Alternate wet and dry materials, such as green grass clippings and hay. If you use many different materials, your compost will contain a wide variety of nutrients.

5. Spread a 2-inch layer of manure over the layer of plant materials to provide an adequate supply of nitrogen. The bacteria will use the nitrogen to decompose the plant materials. Cottonseed meal or other materials which contain nitrogen can be used instead of manure. Do not use commercial fertilizer.

6. Spread a *thin* layer (about 1/8 inch) of rich topsoil mixed with a light sprinkling of wood ash or limestone. Too much soil will hinder air circulation. Rich soil contributes bacteria and other organisms to the compost heap. Wood ash or limestone helps neutralize acidity and provides additional nutrients. (If you are using phosphate rock or bone meal in the compost heap, mix it in this layer.)

7. Moisten the layers thoroughly, if needed, until the materials feel as moist as a damp sponge or towel which has been wrung out. It is best to moisten the compost heap as you build it, so that the moisture throughout the heap is fairly consistent. Be careful not to saturate the heap.

8. Begin a series of layers again. Spread a thick layer of dry weeds and sawdust or a mixture of other plant materials.

9. Spread a layer of kitchen waste which has been accumulated in a tight-lidded container. Sawdust in the bottom of the kitchen waste container helps to absorb juices. As you accumulate kitchen scraps, sprinkle limestone or wood ash occasionally, and empty the container often to help prevent odor and discourage flies from laying their eggs.

10. Add a layer of manure.
11. Cover the manure with a thin layer of soil.
12. Moisten the new layers of the compost heap.

13. Continue layering the compost materials until the heap is 3 to 5 feet high.   Combine different textures and alternate wet and dry materials. You can use any combination of materials you choose as long as your compost heap is made of approximately 2/3 plant material and 1/3 manure.   The heap needs to be at least 3 feet high for it to be large enough to retain heat. A heap which is higher than 5 feet tends to compress and prevent air circulation in the lower portion of the heap.
14. Cover the finished compost heap with a layer of soil and a thick layer of hay for insulation.
15. Lightly press the top of the compost heap to form a shallow basin to catch rainfall.   In an area with heavy rainfall, leave the heap rounded on top.  If your compost heap is contained in a wooden bin, you can remove and replace the roof to regulate watering, catching rainfall as needed.   Rain is a saturated solution of oxygen and contains microorganisms and many minerals, especially near the sea.   Water the compost heap with a hose when there is not enough rainfall.

## CARING FOR YOUR COMPOST HEAP

Your compost heap will heat up quickly and settle in 4 or 5 days. A 5-foot heap settles to approximately 3 1/2 feet. Remove the wooden poles at this time: Move the poles back and forth in the heap to compress the materials around the holes. If this is done, the holes are more likely to remain when you pull the poles out. Perforated drainage pipes and cylinders of chicken wire can be left in the compost heap, as there is a way for the air to circulate down the holes and into the heap.

A good way to find out if your compost heap is working well is to reach into the center of the heap with your hands. The materials should feel moist and very warm. If you notice steam coming from the aeration holes or the top surface of the heap, there is no question that the materials are decomposing.

After approximately 3 weeks, turn the compost heap (inside out). A pitchfork is the best tool to use. Move the materials on the outside of the heap to the center of the new heap and the materials originally in the center to the outside. If your compost heap is contained in a bin, ask a friend to help you lift the bin from around the compost materials and move it to a place nearby. Push the wooden poles into the loosened soil of the new composting area. Then fork the compost materials into the bin, "fluffing" them to ensure air penetration. Water the materials as you turn the compost heap, if they are not moist.

Turning the compost heap mixes and aerates the mass of materials. Turning exposes all the materials in the heap to the high temperatures of the interior.

Turn the compost heap again about 5 weeks after the first turning. The wooden poles are no longer needed for vertical aeration. The compost is ready to use about 3 months from the time the heap is first completed (or 4 weeks after the second turning). This time period is based on Albert Howard's work in the warm climate of Indore, India. Composting in colder climates may require a longer period for decomposition.

## OTHER WAYS OF TENDING YOUR HEAP

You can turn the compost heap each week. The more frequently you turn the heap, the more rapidly it decomposes.

You can choose not to turn the compost heap at all. Compost can be made without turning, although the materials can take as long as a year to decompose. More space is needed to accommodate other compost heaps that you build during the year. Without turning, it is likely that the conditions in the heap will become primarily anaerobic. If the odor of the compost heap becomes annoying, you can either turn the heap to aerate it or cover it to prevent the circulation of air completely.

## POSSIBLE PROBLEMS AND HOW TO SOLVE THEM

| Problem | Cause | Solution |
|---|---|---|
| The compost heap does not heat up. | Too wet: The compost materials are soggy. | Turn the heap, adding dry, absorbent material, like sawdust. |
| | Too dry: There hasn't been enough rainfall to moisten the heap thoroughly. | Water the heap with a hose. Be sure the water penetrates the heap, without saturating it. |
| | Not enough nitrogen: The compost heap is moist, but isn't decomposing. The heap contains too much material which is high in carbon, like straw and sawdust. | Turn the heap, adding a material rich in nitrogen, like manure or cottonseed meal. |
| The compost heap has a putrid odor (like rotten eggs). | Too wet/not enough oxygen: Your compost heap is putrefying, rather than decomposing. Anaerobic organisms release smelly substances. | Turn the heap to aerate it and add dry, absorbent material. |

| Problem | Cause | Solution |
|---|---|---|
| The compost heap has an odor of ammonia. | Too much nitrogen:  Excess nitrogen is released to the atmosphere in the form of ammonia gas. | Turn the heap and add sawdust or another material high in carbon. The carbon will balance the amount of nitrogen in the heap. |
| | Too alkaline:  The loss of nitrogen in the form of ammonia increases when the compost heap is very alkaline (high pH).  Adding too much limestone to the heap can make it too alkaline. | Turn the heap, adding an acid material like sawdust, oak leaves, or kitchen garbage. |
| | Too wet/not enough oxygen:  Anaerobic conditions also produce a smell of ammonia. | Turn the heap, adding dry, absorbent material. |

# 10. SPECIAL COMPOSTS

Special compost mixtures can be made to meet particular plant needs: Composts made of oak leaves, sawdust, kitchen garbage, and cottonseed meal can be used for plants which prefer an acid soil, like strawberries or blueberries. Tomato plants grow especially well in compost made from their own residues.

Coarse, woody compost materials can be placed in a separate compost heap. This rough heap is built in the same way as a regular compost heap, although a much longer period of decomposition is needed. Since the hard-to-decompose materials are composted separately, it is easier to sift the compost of your regular heaps. The materials from a rough heap can be used to activate another compost heap. Composted separately and composted again in a regular heap, the hard-to-decompose materials are given at least twice the usual amount of time for decomposition.

Mushroom compost is the source of food energy for mushrooms. Unlike green plants, mushrooms cannot manufacture any of their own food. Mushrooms need an abundance of decaying organic matter to grow and develop.

Strawy horse manure, commonly used in mushroom grow-ing for many years, makes an excellent mushroom compost. Mushroom compost can be made by combining straw with fresh horse manure.  The straw should be moistened thor-oughly several days before mixing it with the manure.  Manure which contains a liberal amount of straw can be placed di-rectly in a heap for composting.  Manure which has been mixed with wood shavings or sawdust is too acid to be used for mushroom compost. Other kinds of manure, like chicken or rabbit, can also be used for the compost.

As you build the compost heap, sprinkle gypsum (about 20 pounds for 1/2 ton of manure) over the straw and manure mixture.[1]  The gypsum provides calcium and helps keep the compost loose and aerated.  Turn the compost heap every 5 or 6 days, moistening the materials as needed.[2]  After 3 or 4 turnings, the compost is ready to be used.  It is important that the compost heats up well to eliminate any organisms potentially harmful to the mushrooms.  A half ton of com-post will provide 60 square feet of growing space (from which you can harvest about 100 pounds of mushrooms).[3]

# 11. USING YOUR COMPOST

Scoop up a handful of your compost. It should feel loose and crumbly. The compost should be a dark brown color and smell earthy and pleasant. Look closely at the compost in your hand. Some of the organic materials have decomposed completely and turned to *humus*—the dark uniform-looking substance of the compost. You will be able to distinguish little pieces of straw, cornstalk, or eggshell which have not broken down completely. Added to your soil, this organic matter will continue to decompose, releasing its nutrients gradually. The compost you have made will substantially enrich your garden soil.

If your compost contains many materials which have not broken down and is very fibrous, allow it to mature longer. You can leave the compost in the heap or add it to the soil. Do not plant immediately after you add half-decomposed compost to the soil. If you plant too soon, before the compost materials have decayed further, the plants will suffer from nitrogen hunger. The microorganisms use nitrogen from the soil to decompose the compost materials. When the compost is decomposed, nitrogen is gradually released back into the soil as the microorganisms die and decompose.

## ADDING COMPOST TO YOUR SOIL

Loosen your garden soil.  By using a spading fork, you can loosen and aerate clay soil without subsoil clods being brought to the surface.  Spread a layer of compost at least 1 to 3 inches deep and lightly mix it with the topsoil.  Use compost liberally.  Compost will not burn the plants, as commercial fertilizers do when too much is used.  One or 2 pounds of compost (1 cubic yard of compost weighs approximately 1,000 pounds) for every 2 square feet of soil will support the growth of an abundant, healthy crop of vegetables and fruits.

## USING COMPOST IN SEED FLATS OR COLD FRAMES

Compost used for germinating seeds needs to be of a fine texture.  The texture of compost which has been sifted through a screen is ideal for planting seeds or young plants. A simple sifter can be made of a wooden frame with a 1/4-inch mesh screen attached to one side.  The materials which are sifted out can be used in the bottom of the seed flats to provide drainage or as an activator in other compost heaps. For cold frame soil, mix 1 part sifted compost with 1 part sand and 2 parts rich soil.  For seed flats, mix equal parts of compost, sand, and soil or create your own planting mixture. Allow the mixture to age for several months before planting the seeds.

## COMPOST AS A MULCH OR TOP-DRESSING

Compost, partially decomposed or matured, can be used as a mulch (see chapter 12) or top-dressing around growing plants. Lightly cultivate the soil and spread a layer of compost around the plants. When fertilizing trees with compost, spread a ring of compost around the trunk. Begin about 2 feet from the tree trunk and spread the compost 1 foot beyond the drip line of the tree leaves. A thick layer (2 to 3 inches) of compost will conserve soil moisture and provide plants with additional nutrients.

## TRANSPLANTING WITH COMPOST

Compost increases the survival rate of transplants by helping the soil retain moisture and supplying essential nutrients. Apply mature, sifted compost liberally around the roots of transplants. Spread a 1- or 2-inch layer over the soil surface after the plant is in place.

## COMPOST AND HOUSE PLANTS

Sifted compost, combined with equal parts of rich soil and sand, makes a good potting soil mixture. Special potting mixtures of oak leaf or pine needle compost can be made for acid-loving plants. Older house plant soil can be rejuvenated by adding a thin layer of sifted compost and lightly scratching it into the soil surface.

## COMPOST TEA

To keep your house plants happy feed them every 2 weeks with compost tea. Compost tea is made by steeping a cheesecloth bag of compost in a small bucket of water until the water turns the color of weak tea. Compost tea can also be used to water plants which have been recently transplanted.

## COMPOST AND LAWNS

When putting in a new lawn, mix a liberal amount of compost into the soil to a depth of 6 inches or more. Use compost to rejuvenate a patchy lawn: Dig up the bare spots and mix in compost to a depth of about 2 inches. Tamp, rake, and moisten the areas thoroughly, and then sow the grass seed. Use compost to feed your lawn each spring: Spread a layer of fine-textured compost over the entire lawn, being careful not to smother the grass by covering it completely.[1]

# MULCHING, SHEET COMPOSTING, AND GREEN MANURE COMPOSTING

*Mulching* is a way of composting directly on the land. The main difference between mulching and composting is that the organic materials used in mulching are not exposed to the high temperatures characteristic of compost heaps. Mulch is a layer of material which covers the soil surface.

Mulching benefits your garden soil and plants in many ways: Mulching conserves soil moisture by reducing evaporation. The soil is insulated from extreme temperature fluctuations, keeping the plant roots warm in cold weather and cool in hot weather. Mulch protects the soil from pounding raindrops, controlling soil erosion. Mulch keeps the plants clean and dry, protecting the fruits of melons, squashes, strawberries, and tomatoes from mildew and rotting. The need for weeding and cultivating is nearly eliminated, due to the fact that mulch controls the growth of weeds by depriving them of sunlight. Soil underneath an area which has been mulched is kept moist and loose. As the mulch decomposes, it contributes organic matter and nutrients to the soil. Earthworms feed on the underside of the mulch, mixing it with earth in their rich castings. The more you mulch, the more worms there are helping to condition your soil.

Most of the organic materials used in a compost heap are good mulches:  "Spoiled" hay, weeds, dry grass clippings, chopped leaves, rotted sawdust, nutshells, wood chips, strawy manure, and partially decomposed compost.  Fine-textured materials, like sawdust and coffee grounds, should be combined with other materials because they compact when wet. Pine needles are particularly good for plants which like acid soil, such as strawberries.  Materials like black plastic can be used for mulching, but mulches which decompose, contributing organic matter and nutrients to the soil, are more worthwhile.  Mulch materials which are high in carbon content, like straw and sawdust, and which have not been weathered and partially decomposed should be supplemented with a source of nitrogen.  Without additional nitrogen, the microorganisms decomposing these mulch materials will use the soil nitrogen, depriving the plants of this essential nutrient.  Treat the soil with cottonseed meal, manure, or other materials high in nitrogen before spreading this kind of mulch.

Condition your soil with compost before mulching, rather than assuming that the mulch will take care of conditioning your soil for you. The mulch will help maintain soil fertility, continually decomposing and contributing organic matter and nutrients. Composting and mulching are important for soil conditioning and fertility. Before spreading the mulch around your plants, moisten the soil. Keep the mulch materials moist: When rainfall is light and the mulch is dry, little moisture penetrates to the soil surface and below. Although the need for watering is reduced dramatically when mulch is used, it is important to check the soil underneath periodically and water when dry. Vary the materials you use for mulching. When a layer of mulch decomposes and needs to be replenished, use a different material to replace it. The various mulch materials contribute different nutrients to the soil.

*Sheet composting* is similar to mulching in that organic materials are spread over the soil surface. In sheet composting, manure, leaves, green grass clippings, and other raw materials are worked into the soil with a spade or rotary tiller (preferably one with rear tines). Fall is a good time to prepare a planting area by sheet composting. The materials will decompose in time for spring planting. No vegetable crops should be planted and grown in the soil while the materials are decomposing.

*Green manure composting* is the most practical method for conditioning and fertilizing the soil of large gardens or farms. Organic materials do not have to be collected and spread over the garden as in sheet composting. The organic material needed is grown right on the land and then turned into the soil. Planted in late summer or fall, these *cover crops* (a list of green manure or cover crops can be found in Appendix II) can protect your soil during winter, preventing erosion. Nutrients in the soil are absorbed and stored in the growing plants, lessening the possibility of their loss through leaching during rains. Plant roots are an important source of organic matter in the deeper layers of the soil. The roots of cover crops help to loosen the soil and bring up minerals from soil depths. These minerals are made available to shallow-rooted plants when the cover crop is turned under and decomposes in the surface layers of the soil.

Legumes like alfalfa, clover, vetch, bean, and pea are good cover crops, adding substantial nitrogen to the soil. Legume plants have <u>Rhizobium</u> bacteria living in nodules on their roots. The bacteria obtain food from the root cells of the plant. These bacteria are capable of "fixing" nitrogen from the air and converting it to a form of nitrogen which plants can use. When the plant is cut or turned under, the nodules drop off the roots and release the nitrogen they contain into the soil.

In Alabama a study was made comparing the value of vetch with that of commercial nitrogen. During a 6-year period, an average of only 3 bushels of snap beans were harvested when neither green manure nor nitrogen was used. Snap beans planted in soil fertilized with a green manure crop of vetch produced 161 bushels. This was better than the results obtained with commercial nitrogen. Sixty pounds of chemical fertilizer per acre produced 144 bushels of beans.[1]

Root nodules produced by Rhizobium bacteria on a 5- to 6-week-old pea seedling (Pisum sativum). (Reprinted from *The Unseen World*, by René J. Dubas, 1963. Permission granted by The Rockefeller University Press.)

After harvesting your food crops, turn the stalks or vines under, mixing them into the soil. Sow the seeds of your green manure crop, broadcasting them evenly over the planting area. Use a rake to lightly cover the seeds with soil. Firm and moisten the seedbed to aid in germination. After several weeks, your cover crop will be established in the soil. Before the plants flower and mature, becoming woody, turn the crop into the soil with a rotary tiller. After about 6 weeks, the cover crop is sufficiently decomposed for you to plant a food crop. A cover crop can be grown and turned under 4 or 5 times a year or it can be mowed or grazed and allowed to grow several times before being tilled in.[2] Whenever possible, it is good to add other organic materials to the soil as well. Green manure and crop residues should be supplemented to provide maximum soil conditioning.

The basis of green manuring is to provide the soil with succulent organic matter at the peak of its nutritional benefit. If the crop is allowed to mature, it has a greater proportion of carbohydrate and adds a greater bulk of organic matter, but needs additional nitrogen for decomposition.[3] Generally, if green manure crops are rotated with food crops, plant diseases and insects are discouraged. (Fava beans are an especially good cover crop to use before planting tomatoes, helping to eradicate tomato wilt organisms.[4] )

# 13. MICROSCOPIC COMPOSTERS

An effective compost heap provides a good environment for the microorganisms and other soil life which decompose organic matter. A large proportion of humus consists of living, dead, and decomposing microorganism bodies. The remaining proportion consists of plant and animal residues, which have decomposed as a result of the activities of the microorganisms. Without bacteria and other soil life, leaves, grasses, fruits, and other organic materials which collect on the earth's surface would never decompose. These tiny organisms are the earth's composters, recycling the vital elements needed for continued life.

The various microorganisms work in different ways in the compost heap and the soil. Each kind of organism plays a particular role in the decomposition of plant and animal matter. The microorganisms help to make nutrients available to plants and develop soil structure. As conditions in the compost heap change, the character of the population of microorganisms also changes.

## BACTERIA, FUNGI, AND ACTINOMYCETES

*Bacteria* are one-celled, microscopic organisms present in almost all natural environments, often in extremely large numbers. There can be several billion bacteria in a gram of rich garden soil. Bacteria are among the smallest living organisms known. One of the periods on this page would cover about 250,000 average-sized bacteria.

When conditions are favorable, bacteria grow rapidly. Some bacteria can reproduce approximately every 15 minutes. Bacteria characteristically reproduce asexually. Each cell divides into two new cells by a process called *binary fission*. Every 15 minutes, a population of bacteria can double: One cell divides into 2. The cell elongates, becomes pinched in at the midpoint, and the 2 new cells separate. Then the process begins again. Fifteen minutes later, the 2 cells divide into 4 and so on. The availability of food energy (from nutrients of the various organic materials in the compost heap), temperature, oxygen supply, and moisture determine how large the population grows.

*Fungi* are everywhere and in very large numbers, particularly where organic matter is plentiful. There are about 1 million fungi in a gram of rich garden soil. Together with bacteria, fungi decompose organic matter and release the essential elements that otherwise would be forever locked up in the dead bodies of plants and animals.

A typical fungus consists of a mass of branched, threadlike filaments, collectively known as the *mycelium*. The mycelium obtains food from organic matter in the soil (or compost heap) and grows outward, just below the surface. Upon reaching a certain stage of maturity, certain types of fungi form mushrooms, which appear above the soil surface. Mushrooms are the fruiting bodies of these fungi, containing spores, or reproductive "seeds." When a spore is released and lands in a favorable spot, it germinates and grows into a filament. The filament branches and becomes the mycelium of the new fungus.

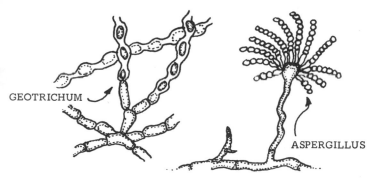

GEOTRICHUM

ASPERGILLUS

*Actinomycetes* are funguslike bacteria, widely distributed in nature. There are perhaps 10 to 20 million actinomycetes in a gram of soil. The characteristic "earthy" odor of freshly turned soil is due to substances produced by actinomycetes. Many actinomycetes excrete vitamins, growth substances, and antibiotics. Actinomycetes aid in the decomposition of plant and animal material.

Actinomycetes

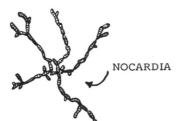

NOCARDIA

MICROMONOSPORA

STREPTOMYCES

# 14. THE EARTHWORM

The earthworm is one of the earth's composters, working with bacteria and other organisms to decompose the organic materials deposited on the earth's surface. Earthworms condition the soil: They aerate the soil with the tunnels they build, providing space and nutrients for growing plant roots. Soil which has been worked by earthworms is porous and spongelike, absorbing rainfall readily. Earthworms pull leaves and other organic materials below the earth's surface, digesting and mixing them with the soil. Subsoil minerals are brought up and mixed with the surface layers of the soil. Earthworms continually release nutrients from mineral soil and organic matter, making them available to plants. Tons of soil per acre are ploughed, cultivated, and fertilized each year by earthworms. The presence of earthworms is an indication of living, productive soil.

As an earthworm moves through the soil or compost heap, it swallows and digests bits of leaves, straw, and other organic materials: Three pairs of glands excrete calcium carbonate (lime), neutralizing acids contained in the organic materials. The gizzard grinds the food into smaller pieces with the help of very small stones and sand swallowed by the worm.

From the gizzard, the food is moved through the intestine, and undigested food is expelled as castings. An earthworm can produce its weight in castings every 24 hours—up to 1/2 pound of castings each year. Approximately 3 inches of new topsoil from castings is deposited by worms every 15 years. The castings of an earthworm are very fertile: They contain 5 times the nitrogen content of the surrounding soil, 7 times the phosphorus, 11 times the potassium, 3 times the magnesium, and 2 times the calcium of the soil.

The earthworms commonly found in manure and compost are rather short, thick, and reddish in appearance. Soon after your compost heap is built, these red worms will begin to grow, multiply, and feed on the organic compost materials. If you do not feel that your population of worms is large enough, you can supply additional red worms to the compost heap. (Earthworms can be purchased from a local worm grower or through the mail from large nursery suppliers. Gardening and fishing magazines carry advertisements for mail-order sales of earthworms.) Wait about 3 weeks, until the initial heat in the compost heap subsides. Then make several holes in the compost heap and put 50 to 100 worms in each. The earthworms work to decompose the compost materials until they are turned to humus and the compost is mature. When there is no more food, the worms die and decompose, adding nitrogen to the compost. When you spread compost on your soil, long, thin, blue-grey worms begin to work and decompose the organic matter. Occasionally, these blue-grey soil worms migrate into a compost heap which is nearly mature to further decompose the organic materials.

Earthworms multiply very rapidly if in a favorable environment. One of the most important things you can do for earthworms is to feed them. Be sure that your soil contains plenty of organic matter. Compost and mulch provide good food for earthworms, as well as your plants. Earthworms need moisture and warmth to work and multiply. Mulch keeps the soil moist and protects it from extreme temperature fluctuation. Earthworms will help keep the soil pH near neutral, but only if your soil is not too acid or alkaline to begin with. Do not disturb the soil too frequently by hoeing or tilling. The earthworms will do much of this work for you, particularly if not disturbed often.

Organic matter and mineral rock fragments are the earthworm's natural food. If you use strong chemical fertilizers in your soil, the population of earthworms will diminish rapidly. Ammonium sulfate, a fertilizer used by many farmers, is particularly harmful to earthworms. It has even been recommended for such uses as killing earthworms on golf course greens. Strong insect sprays are even more destructive to earthworms. Where earthworms are scarce, the earth becomes hard-packed and difficult to cultivate. Birds move away because of the lack of their usual food—the earthworm. The land and vegetation suffer further because there are fewer birds to destroy large amounts of noxious insects and their larvae. . . .[1]   Treat earthworms kindly, and they will help you keep your soil fertile.

## EARTHWORM BOX COMPOSTING

During the cold winter months, when it is difficult to work outside, you can easily turn household garbage into rich compost in your basement or garage. With the help of earthworms, compost can be made in boxes.

Ask for several fruit or vegetable lug boxes at a local food market or build your own earthworm box. A large earthworm box can be built from 1 sheet of 4- by 8-foot plywood: Saw 1-foot pieces from each end of the plywood, as well as 1-foot pieces from each side. You now have a bottom for the box which has dimensions of 2 by 6 feet. Nail the 6-foot-long side pieces to the bottom of the box. Cut a 4-foot end piece in half and nail each piece to the box to enclose the ends. Drill 1/2-inch holes in the bottom of the box and some around the sides to provide aeration and drainage. Set the earthworm box on concrete blocks or several sawhorses. Spread a layer of small rocks or gravel in the bottom of the box.

Order 2,000 to 3,000 "bed-run" (mixed ages) worms (or 1/2 pound for each fruit lug box). Now you are ready to prepare bedding for the earthworms, so it will be ready when they arrive. The bedding must be of a material which will remain moist and porous. Aged horse manure and compost are good bedding materials to use. Sprinkle ground limestone over the bedding material to neutralize any acidity. Moisten the materials thoroughly and spread a 4- to 5-inch layer in the box. Be sure that the materials are no longer heating up when you add the worms. Earthworms will not thrive in bedding which has a temperature much higher than 27°C (80°F) or 32°C (90°F).

To add the earthworms to the box, push aside some bedding in several places in the box (or in the center of a smaller box) and gently cover the worms.   Place a loose-fitting cover over the box to keep it dark, warm, and moist.

After several days, begin to feed kitchen garbage to the worms.   You can add up to 1 pound of garbage to the box each day.   Chop the materials with a knife or in a blender to make it easier for the worms to feed.   Push aside enough bedding to make a hole for the garbage and cover it with some of the bedding.   The following day, put the garbage in another part of the box.   Each addition of garbage is consumed in 3 or 4 days.

Keep the bedding in the earthworm box moist.   If excess water drains out of the bottom of the box, collect it in a container and use it to water your house plants.   After approximately 1 month, the population of earthworms will have doubled and will need several more inches of bedding. When the earthworm box is full, remove half of the compost and spread it in several small piles on a tarp in bright light. The worms, disliking bright light, will cluster together in the bottom of the piles.   Add them to another earthworm box or to your compost heap.   The earthworm castings can be added to your garden soil, spread on your lawn (1/2 inch thick), or used for indoor planting mix.

# 15. COMMUNITY COMPOSTING

The problem of community wastes is very serious. We are currently producing 135,000,000 tons of solid waste every year in the United States alone. The most common method used to dispose of this huge amount of waste material is sanitary landfilling. Put more simply, we are burying it. But sanitary landfill is becoming increasingly expensive, hazardous, and generally impractical: We are running out of land near the cities in which we can dispose of waste. Such land that is still available is increasingly expensive. Sanitary landfills are extremely hazardous to the environment: Water passing through a landfill, from rainfall or other sources, becomes polluted. This water can in turn pollute the underground water table or nearby rivers and streams. In some landfills, methane gas, which is highly explosive, can build up, creating the hazard of fire or explosion. Landfill areas which have been converted to parks or used as building sites have been known to settle, causing damage to property and hazard to life.[1]

We are wasting valuable resources. We can create a highly useful material by composting community wastes. Composting is the only method of solid waste disposal which does not cause contamination of water or pollution of the atmosphere, and does not abuse the land. Resources are conserved directly by returning to the land the nutrients contained in the refuse, thus preserving and restoring the environment.[2] Composting can be a solution to the waste disposal problem, accommodating the social and economic needs of many communities.

Community composting requires that waste be separated into materials which are biodegradable and those which are not.   The easiest way of doing this is to keep the biodegradable waste separate from the beginning.   This requires that individual households are cooperative and take the responsibility of separating their own wastes.   Some of the resources, such as metal, glass, and paper, can be recycled in community centers.   Before composting, the waste materials need to be shredded or ground in order to hasten decomposition and produce a uniform material.   The materials can then be composted in open piles, or windrows, or in digesters.

A compost plant in Houston receives approximately 2,000 tons of refuse each week—100,000 tons per year.   Approximately 2/3 of this tonnage is composted.   The plant operates 6 days per week—2 shifts with about 25 workers each 8-hour shift.   The plant is located alongside a railroad siding so that salvage material can be loaded directly into freight cars. Aluminum, brass, tires, heavy plastics, and other nonferrous materials (containing no iron) are removed manually, since they are not picked up later by the magnetic separator. Large hunks of iron and steel, which can damage the grinding mills, are also removed.[3]

Refuse is collected from the community and taken to the composting plant. The materials are pushed onto a conveyor belt which leads to a sorting area. Generally 6 workers on a side remove salvage materials manually. The materials move on the conveyor to a 500-horsepower hammer mill, where they are ground up. The refuse then moves into one of 4 digestion tanks. The material usually stays in the digester for 4 days, after which it is stockpiled outdoors until distribution.[4]

Another method for converting community wastes into usable material is through the help of earthworms. This method, called *annelidic consumption,* is already in use on a commercial scale in both Japan and Canada. A project in Ontario, California (Annelidic Consumption Programs, North American Bait Farms, 1207 South Palmetto, Ontario, California 91761) is determining if earthworms can consume biodegradable waste materials in multiton lots, with feasible land, water, and energy requirements. The earthworm castings can be sold to nurseries or farmers, providing income which can offset a considerable portion of the operating costs.

## SEWAGE SLUDGE

Nearly every community with a population over 2,500 operates a sewage disposal plant. Most of these communities make the sewage sludge available to any farmer or gardener who chooses to use it. Sewage sludge, containing plant nutrients and organic matter, can be used as a soil conditioner and as an activator in composting. Sludge is used to restore areas which have been despoiled by strip mining. Many municipal parks use sludge for the upkeep of their lawns and other vegetation.

Sewage is generally processed either by digestion (anaerobic) or activation (agitated by air rapidly bubbling through it). Activated sludge, which is heat treated, is a good organic fertilizer. It has a relatively high nitrogen content and is generally free of harmful organisms. However, some caution is needed in using sewage sludge in home gardens: Some sludges contain a large amount of metals, such as zinc and copper, as well as pollutants, like detergents and pesticide residues.

Sewage sludge can be used very effectively in community composting as an activator in municipal refuse composting or in composting of industrial wastes, such as wood chips and sawdust. A method developed by the USDA (United States Department of Agriculture) center in Beltsville, Maryland, can process 600 tons of sludge per day: Wood chips (15 inches deep) are placed on a paved area (15 feet wide) and heat-treated sludge is spread over the chips at a ratio of 3 to 1 by volume. The sludge and chips are mixed by machine and formed into long windrows. The windrows are turned at certain intervals (perhaps 5 times a week) over a period of 3 weeks. The end result is a compost beneficial to the land.[5]

## ANIMAL WASTES

Composting can also be used as a way to handle the tremendous quantity (2 billion tons per year) of animal wastes produced by cattle and poultry farms. Surface and ground water pollution and other disposal problems of the accumulated waste, can be alleviated by composting. If animal wastes are composted, large amounts of nitrogen and other nutrients are conserved. The composted wastes can be incorporated into the land without serious detriment to the ecosystem.

Manure has sufficient nitrogen to make good compost easily. It can be mixed with straw, corncobs, sawdust, wood chips, shredded paper, leaves, cannery wastes, and various other materials. The use of straw or wood shavings as animal bedding provides a good mixture for composting.

## LEAVES

Leaves and tree trimmings accumulated by communities can be composted as a public service. Cities such as Toronto, Ontario; Portland, Oregon; Scarsdale, New York; and Maplewood, New Jersey, collect, shred, and compost community leaves. The finished compost is supplied to anyone interested. The compost can be incorporated into the soil, used as a mulch in vegetable or flower gardens and around trees, or used as a straight planting medium for root crops such as potatoes. And so an age-old principle is modified to operate successfully on an urban scale.

# 16. COMPOSTING TOILETS

Your involvement in recycling wastes can include recycling your own body wastes. Human wastes, mixed with kitchen garbage, garden wastes, and air, can be effectively composted in your home. The process used is similar to the one operating in your compost heap. The valuable nutrients in your body waste can be returned to the soil. People in Asia have been composting human wastes for centuries, using the compost to maintain the fertility of their land.

The standard flush toilet uses a tremendous amount of fresh water to carry away a relatively small amount of body waste. Although you may flush the toilet and feel that the "problem" has been sufficiently disposed of, in reality your wastes are contributing to water and land pollution. City sewage systems are costly and generally require a large amount of energy and water to treat the wastes. Disposal of the huge volume of sewage sludge presents an environmental problem.

The composting toilet is a water-saving alternative to the standard flush toilet. Several models of composting toilets are available in the United States and Canada.

Large composting toilets, like the Clivus Multrum and the Toa Throne, have few moving parts and use very little, if any, electricity. The large, inclined container, designed to sit underneath the bathroom floor, allows good air circulation and handles large amounts of waste materials. When you dispose of wastes down the chute, they spread out and mix with the other organic materials in the container. Air enters the bottom of the container through small holes and is drawn up through the mass of waste materials and out long, insulated ventilation pipes. This circulation of *warm* air, at least 18°C (65°F), is essential for the evaporation of liquid wastes. The heat generated by aerobic decomposition maintains the temperature inside the tank at approximately 24°C (75°F). The installation of a heat exchanger in the ventilation pipe can recycle heat otherwise lost from the house, and heat from the decomposition process.

Before the composting toilet can be used, you need to spread a layer of organic materials, such as peat moss, compost, and rich garden soil, over the bottom of the container. These absorbent materials add bulk and introduce the necessary bacteria for decomposition. During the first year of use, you will need to add a large amount of organic materials high in carbon. It is necessary to add these materials in order to build up enough mass to maintain sufficient heat.

Once the decomposition process is stabilized, you need only add waste materials to maintain your composting toilet. You also need to be aware of any problems as they occur, so that they can be easily corrected. After 2 or 3 years of use, the compost storage chamber can be emptied. It is often recommended that the compost be placed in a regular compost heap for 6 months before being used, to be certain that all pathogenic organisms are eliminated. The finished compost can be used in your vegetable garden and everywhere that you would normally use the compost from your regular heaps.

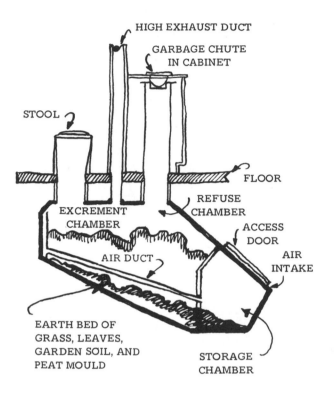

The Clivus Multrum Composting Toilet.

The Clivus Multrum is a well-known composting toilet developed in Sweden in 1939. The Clivus composting unit consists of a large, slanting tank connected to separate incoming toilet and kitchen waste chutes and an outgoing air vent. Although the unit is relatively expensive and difficult to install because of its size, it conserves water, is odor-free, and can handle large amounts of waste.

Smaller composting toilets, such as the Mullbank, Mull-Toa, Soddy Potty #2, and the Bio Loo, are also available. These units are easier to install, but do not hold a large enough mass of materials to retain sufficient heat for effective decomposition and need another source of heat. In addition, all the units include a ventilation fan to assure good air circulation. These composting toilets have a smaller holding capacity and need to be emptied at least once or twice a year, depending on the number of people using them. The compost must be placed in a regular compost heap for 6 months before being used in a vegetable garden.

# APPENDICES

# I. NUTRIENT CONTENT OF VARIOUS MATERIALS

## NITROGEN CONTENT OF ORGANIC SUBSTANCES

The following is a list of representative classifications of organic matter and typical analyse respect to their nitrogen content:

### Meal

| | |
|---|---|
| Bone Black Bone Meal | 1.5 |
| Raw Bone Meal | 3.3 to 4.1 |
| Steamed Bone Meal | 1.6 to 2.5 |
| Cottonseed Meal | 7.0 |
| Corn Fodder | 0.41 |
| Oats, Green Fodder | 0.49 |
| Corn Silage | 0.42 |
| Gluten Meal | 6.4 |
| Wheat Bran | 2.36 |
| Wheat Middlings | 2.75 |
| Meat Meal | 9 to 11 |
| Bone Tankage | 3 to 10 |

### Manures

| | |
|---|---|
| Cattle Manure (solid fresh excrement) | 0.29 |
| Cattle Manure (fresh urine) | 0.58 |
| Hen Manure (fresh) | 1.63 |
| Dog Manure | 2.0 |
| Horse Manure (solid fresh excrement) | 0.44 |
| Horse Manure (fresh urine) | 1.55 |
| Human Excrement (solid) | 1.00 |
| Human Urine | 0.60 |
| Night Soil | 0.80 |
| Sheep Manure (solid fresh excrement) | 0.55 |
| Sheep (fresh urine) | 1.95 |
| Stable Manure, mixed | 0.50 |
| Swine Manure (solid fresh excrement) | 0.60 |
| Swine (fresh urine) | 0.43 |
| Sewage Sludge | 1.7 to 2.26 |

### Animal Wastes (Other than manures)

| | |
|---|---|
| Eggshells | 1.00 + |
| Dried Blood | 10 to 14 |
| Feathers | 15.3 |
| Dried Jellyfish | 4.6 |
| Fresh Crabs | 5.0 |
| Dried Ground Crabs | 10.0 |
| Dried Shrimp Heads | 7.8 |
| Lobster Wastes | 2.9 |
| Shrimp Wastes | 2.9 |
| Mussels | 1.0 |
| Dried Ground Fish | 8.0 |
| Acid Fish Scrap | 4.0 to 6.5 |
| Oyster Shells | 0.36 |
| Milk | 0.5 |
| Wool Wastes | 3.5 to 6.0 |
| Silkworm Cocoons | 10.0 |
| Silk Wastes | 8.0 |
| Felt Wastes | 14.0 |

### Plant Wastes

| | % Ni |
|---|---|
| Beet Wastes | 0.4 |
| Brewery Wastes | 1.0 |
| Castor Pomace | 4.0 |
| Cattail Reeds | 2.0 |
| Cocoa Shell Dust | 1.0 |
| Cocoa Wastes | 2.7 |
| Coffee Wastes | 2.0 |
| Grape Pomace | 1.0 |
| Green Cowpeas | 0.4 |
| Nut Shells | 2.5 |
| Olive Residues | 1.1 |
| Peanut Shells | 3.6 |
| Peanut Shell Ashes | 0.8 |
| Pine Needles | 0.5 |
| Potato Skins | 0.6 |
| Sugar Wastes | 2.0 |
| Tea Grounds | 4.1 |
| Tobacco Stems | 2.5 |
| Tung Oil Pomace | 6.1 |

### Leaves

| | |
|---|---|
| Peach Leaves | 0.9 |
| Oak Leaves | 0.8 |
| Grape Leaves | 0.4 |
| Pear Leaves | 0.7 |
| Apple Leaves | 1.0 |
| Cherry Leaves | 0.6 |
| Raspberry Leaves | 1.3 |
| Garden Pea Vines | 0.2 |

### Grasses

| | |
|---|---|
| Clover | 2.0 |
| Red Clover | 0.5 |
| Vetch Hay | 2.8 |
| Corn Stalks | 0.7 |
| Alfalfa | 2.4 |
| Immature Grass | 1.0 |
| Blue Grass Hay | 1.2 |
| Cowpea Hay | 3.0 |
| Pea Hay | 1.5 |
| Soybean Hay | 1.5 |
| Timothy Hay | 1.1 |
| Salt Hay | 1.0 |
| Millet Hay | 1.2 |

### Seaweed

| | |
|---|---|
| Fresh Seaweed | 0.2 |
| Dry Seaweed | 1.1 |

Reprinted from *The Complete Book of Composting* © 1960 by J. I. Rodale. Perm granted by Rodale Press, Inc., Emmaus, Pa. 18049, p. 208.

# PHOSPHATE SOURCES
## (Other than Phosphate Rock or Bone Meal)

| *Material* | *Phosphoric Acid %* |
|---|---|
| Marine products | |
| Shrimp waste (dried) | 10 |
| Dried ground fish | 7 |
| Lobster refuse | 3.5 |
| Dried blood | 1-5 |
| Tankage | 2 |
| Hoof and horn meal | 2 |
| Wool wastes | 2-4 |
| Cottonseed meal | 2-3 |
| Raw sugar wastes | 8 |
| Rape seed meal | 1-2 |
| Cocoa wastes | 1.5 |
| Castor pomace | 1-2 |
| Silk mill wastes | 1.14 |
| Activated sludge | 2.5-4.0 |
| Manure | |
| Poultry, fresh | 1-1.5 |
| Poultry, dried | 1.5-2.0 |
| Goat and sheep, fresh | 0.6 |
| Goat and sheep, dried | 1.0-1.9 |
| Hog, fresh | 0.45 |
| Horse, fresh | 0.35 |
| Horse, dried | 1.0 |
| Cow, fresh | 0.25 |
| Cow, dried | 1.0 |
| Wood ashes | 1-2 |
| Pea pod wastes (ashed) | 3 |
| Banana residue (ashed) | 2.3-3.3 |
| Apple pomace (ashed skin) | 3 |
| Citrus wastes (orange skins, ashed) | 3 |

Reprinted from *The Complete Book of Composting* © 1960 by J. I. Rodale. Permission granted by Rodale Press, Inc., Emmaus, Pa. 18049, p. 209.

## POTASH SOURCES

Potash Content $(K_2O)\%$

| Materials | |
|---|---|
| Wood ashes (broad leaf) | 10.0 |
| Wood ashes (coniferous) | 6.0 |
| Molasses wastes (curbay) | 3.0 to 4.0 |
| Flyash | 12.0 |
| Tobacco stems | 4.5 to 7.0 |
| Garbage (NYC analysis) | 2.3 to 4.3 |
| Water lily stems | 3.4 |
| Cocoa shell residues | 2.6 |
| Potato tubers | 2.5 |
| Dry potato vines | 1.6 |
| Vegetable wastes | 1.4 |
| Castor pomace | 1.0 to 2.0 |
| Rapeseed meal | 1.0 to 3.0 |
| Cottonseed meal | 1.8 |
| Olive pomace | 1.3 |
| Beet wastes | 0.7 to 4.1 |
| Silk mill wastes | 1.0 |
| Wool wastes | 1.0 to 3.5 |

### Hay Materials

| | |
|---|---|
| Vetch hay | 2.3 |
| Alfalfa hay | 2.1 |
| Kentucky blue grass hay | 2.0 |
| Red clover hay | 2.1 |
| Cowpea hay | 2.3 |
| Timothy hay | 1.4 |
| Soybean hay | 1.2 to 2.3 |
| Salt hay | 0.6 |
| Pea forage | 1.4 |
| Winter rye | 1.0 |
| Immature grass | 1.2 |
| Garden pea vines | 0.7 |
| Weeds | 0.7 |

### Leaves

| | |
|---|---|
| Apple leaves | 0.4 |
| Peach leaves | 0.6 |
| Pear leaves | 0.4 |
| Cherry leaves | 0.7 |
| Raspberry leaves | 0.6 |
| Grape leaves | 0.4 |
| Oak leaves | 0.2 |

### Natural Minerals

Granite dust
Greensand marl
Basalt rock

### Straw

Millet
Buckwheat
Oats
Barley
Rye
Sorghum
Wheat
Corn stover

### Manure

Cow (fresh excrement)
    (dried excrement)
    (fresh urine)
Horse (fresh excrement)
    (dried excrement)
    (fresh urine)
Hog (fresh excrement)
    (fresh urine)
Goat and Sheep
    (fresh excrement)
    (dried excrement)
    (fresh urine)
Chicken (fresh)
    (dried)
Pigeon (fresh)
Duck (fresh)
Goose (fresh)
Dog (fresh)

### Ashed Material

Banana residues (ash)
Pea pods (ash)
Cantaloupe rinds (ash)

Reprinted from *The Complete Book of Composting* © 1960 by J. I. Ro
mission granted by Rodale Press, Inc., Emmaus, Pa. 18049, p. 210.

# II. GREEN MANURE CROPS

| Common Name | | Legume | Soil Preference | Lime Requirements (Low, Medium or High) | Adapted to Soils of Low Fertility | Relative Longevity of Seed | Seeding Rate (lbs. per acre) | Seeding Rate (lbs. per 1000 sq. ft.) | Depth to Cover Seed | N.E. and N.C. States | Southern and S.E. States | Gulf Coast and Florida | Northwestern States | Southwestern States | When to Sow | When to Turn Under | Comments |
|---|---|---|---|---|---|---|---|---|---|---|---|---|---|---|---|---|---|
| | | | | | | | | | | Areas For Which Best Adapted | | | | | | | |
| Alfalfa | | Yes | Dry Loams | L | | Long | 15 | 1 | ½ | • | | | • | | Spring 2nd Year at 1st Blossom | Spring or Early Fall | Fixes nitrogen in soil. Deep roots bring trace elements to surface. |
| Barley | | No | Loams | L | | Long | 100 | 2½ | ¾ | • | | | • | • | Spring<br>Fall | Summer<br>Spring | Not good on sandy or acid soils. Sow spring varieties in north, winter varieties in milder climates. |
| Beans | Mung | Yes | Widely Adaptable | L | • | Short | 70 | 2 | 1 | | • | • | | • | Spring or Summer | Summer or Fall | Warm weather crops. Do not sow until ground is warm and weather is settled. |
| | Soy | Yes | Loams | M | | Short | 90 | 2½ | 1½ | • | • | • | • | • | Spring or Summer | Summer or Fall | |
| | Velvet | Yes | Loams | L | • | Short | 120 | 4 | 2 | | | • | | | Spring or Summer | Summer or Fall | |
| Beggar Weed | | Yes | Sandy Loams | L | • | | 15 | ½ | ½ | | | • | | | Spring or Early Summer | Summer or Fall | Seeding rate is for scarified seed. Treble the amount if unhulled seed is used. |
| Brome Grass, Field | | No | Widely Adaptable | L | | Long | 30 | 1 | ½ | • | | | | | Fall<br>Spring | Spring<br>Fall | Good winter cover. Easy to establish. Hardier than rye. More heat tolerant. |
| Buckwheat | | No | Widely Adaptable | L | • | | 50 | 1½ | ¾ | • | | | • | | Late Spring and Summer | Summer or Fall | Quick growing. Plant only after ground is warm. |
| Bur Clover | | Yes | Heavy Loams | M | | Long | 30 | 1 | ½ | | • | • | • | • | Fall | Spring | Not winter hardy north. One of the best winter crops where mild winters prevail. |
| Chess or Cheat Grass | | No | Loams | L | | Long | 40 | 1 | ¾ | | | | | • | Fall | Spring | |
| Clover | Alsike | Yes | Heavy Loams | M | | Long | 8 | ¼ | ½ | • | | | • | • | Spring<br>Fall | Fall<br>Spring | Less sensitive to soil acidity and poorly drained soils than most clovers. |
| | Crimson | Yes | Loams | M | • | Medium | [illegible] | 1 | ½ | • | • | • | • | • | Fall<br>Spring | Spring<br>Fall | Not winter hardy north. A good winter annual from New Jersey southward. |
| | Subterranean | Yes | Loams | M | | Medium | 30 | 1 | ½ | | • | • | • | • | Fall | Spring | |
| Corn | | No | Widely Adaptable | L | | Medium | 90 | 2½ | 1 | • | • | • | • | • | Spring or Summer | Summer or Fall | Do not sow until ground is warm. |
| Cow-Pea | | Yes | Sandy Loams | L | • | Short | 90 | 2½ | 1½ | | • | • | | • | Late Spring or Early Summer | Summer or Fall | Withstands drought and moderate shade well. Do not sow until weather is warm and settled. |
| Crotalaria | | Yes | Light Loams | L | • | Long | 15 | ½ | ¾ | | • | • | | • | Spring or Summer | Summer or Fall | Does well on acid soils. Resistant to root knot nematode. Sow scarified seed. |
| Fenugreek | | Yes | Loams | L | | Long | 35 | 1 | ½ | | | | | • | Fall | Spring | |
| Guar | | Yes | Widely Adaptable | L | • | Long | 40 | 1½ | 1 | | | | | • | Spring or Early Summer | Summer or Fall | Thrives on warm soils. Do not plant too early. |
| Indigo, Hairy | | Yes | Sandy Loams | L | • | Short | 10 | ½ | ½ | | • | • | | • | Spring or Early Summer | Summer or Fall | |
| Kale, Scotch | | No | Widely Adaptable | H | • | Long | 14 | ¼ | ½ | • | • | • | • | • | Summer or Fall | Spring | Can be eaten after serving as winter cover. In Northern areas interplant with winter rye for protection. Except in deep south, plant in summer for good growth before frost. |
| Lespedeza | Common | Yes | Loams | L | • | Short | 25 | 1 | ½ | | • | | | | Early Spring | Summer or Fall | Easy to establish on hard, badly eroded soils. Good on acid soils of low fertility. |
| | Korean | Yes | Loams | L | • | Short | 25 | 1 | ½ | | • | | | | Early Spring | Summer or Fall | |
| | Sericea | Yes | Loams | L | • | Medium | 25 | 1 | ½ | | • | | | • | Early Spring | Summer or Fall | |
| Lupine | Blue | Yes | Sandy Loams | L | | Short | 100 | 2½ | 1 | | | • | | | Spring<br>Fall | Summer<br>Spring | Good on sour and acid soils. |
| | White | Yes | Sandy Loams | L | | Short | 120 | 2½ | 1 | • | | • | | | Spring<br>Fall | Summer<br>Spring | Less popular than the yellow lupine and blue lupine. |
| | Yellow | Yes | Sandy Loams | L | | Short | 80 | 2 | 1 | • | | • | | | Spring<br>Fall | Summer<br>Spring | |
| Millet | | No | Sandy Loams | L | | Long | 30 | 1 | ½ | • | | | | | Late Spring or Summer | Summer or Fall | Sow only after ground is warm, a week or ten days after normal corn planting time. Fast growing. |
| Mustard, White | | No | Loams | | | | 8 | ¼ | ¼ | • | | | | | Spring | Summer | |

| Common Name | Legume | Soil Preference | Lime Requirements (Low, Medium or High) | Adapted to Soils of Low Fertility | Relative Longevity of Seed | Seeding Rate (lbs. per acre) | Seeding Rate (lbs. per 1000 sq. ft.) | Depth to Cover Seed | N.E. and N.C. States | Southern and S.E. States | Gulf Coast and Florida | Northwestern States | Southwestern States (Areas For Which Best Adapted) | When to Sow | When to Turn Under | Comments |
|---|---|---|---|---|---|---|---|---|---|---|---|---|---|---|---|---|
| Oats | No | Widely Adaptable | L | | Long | 100 | 2½ | 1 | • | • | • | • | • | Spring<br>Fall | Summer or Fall<br>Spring | Winter oats (sown in fall) are suitable only where mild winters prevail. |
| Pea — Field | Yes | Heavy Loams | M | | Short | 90 | 2½ | 1½ | • | • | • | • | • | Early Spring<br>Fall | Summer<br>Spring | Sow in fall only where winters are mild. Distinctly a cool weather crop. |
| Pea — Rough | Yes | Sandy Loams | L | • | Medium | 60 | 1½ | 1 | | • | | | | Fall | Spring | |
| Pea — Tangier | Yes | | M | | Medium | 80 | 2½ | 1 | • | | | | • | Spring | Summer | |
| Rape | No | Loams | L | | | 8 | ¼ | ¼ | • | | | • | | Spring or Summer | Summer or Fall | |
| Rescue Grass | No | Widely Adaptable | L | | Long | 35 | 1 | ¾ | | • | | | • | | | Adapted to mild winters and humid climates. |
| Rye, Spring | No | Widely Adaptable | L | | Long | 90 | 2 | ¾ | • | • | | | | Spring | Summer | |
| Rye, Winter | No | Widely Adaptable | L | | Long | 90 | 2 | ¾ | • | • | | | | Fall | Spring | One of the most important winter cover crops. Can be sown late. |
| Rye-Grass, Italian | No | Widely Adaptable | L | | Long | 35 | 1 | ¾ | • | • | • | • | • | Fall<br>Spring | Spring<br>Summer | An important winter cover crop where winters are mild. In severe climates sow in spring or summer. |
| Sesbania | Yes | Widely Adaptable | L | • | Long | 25 | 1 | ¾ | | • | • | | • | Spring or Summer | Summer or Fall | Quick grower. Is better adapted to wet soils and will grow at higher altitudes than crotalaria. |
| Sorghum | No | Light Loams | | | Long | 90 | 2½ | ¾ | • | • | | | • | Late Spring or Summer | Summer or Fall | Do not sow until ground is warm and weather is settled. More drought resistant than corn. |
| Sudan Grass | No | Widely Adaptable | L | | Long | 35 | 1 | ¾ | • | • | • | • | • | Late Spring or Summer | Summer or Fall | Rapid grower. Do not sow until ground is warm and weather is settled. |
| Sunflower | No | Widely Adaptable | L | | | 20 | ¾ | ¾ | • | • | • | • | • | Spring or Summer | Summer or Fall | Intolerant of acid soils. |
| Sweet-Clover — Common White | Yes | Heavy Loams | H | | Long | 15 | ½ | ½ | • | • | | • | • | | | Quite winter hardy. Best results are from fall sowing. |
| Sweet-Clover — Annual (Hubam) | Yes | Loams | H | | Long | 15 | ½ | ½ | • | | | • | | | | A true annual. Best results from spring sowings. |
| Sweet-Clover — Yellow | Yes | Loams | H | | Long | 15 | ½ | ½ | • | • | | • | • | | | Stands dry conditions better than common white sweet clover. |
| Sweet-Clover — Yellow Annual | Yes | Loams | H | | Long | 15 | ½ | ½ | • | • | • | • | • | | | Most useful south of the cotton belt as winter cover. North not winter hardy. Makes short summer growth. |
| Vetch — Common | Yes | Widely Adaptable | L | | Medium | 60 | 1½ | ¾ | • | • | • | • | • | Spring<br>Fall | Fall<br>Spring | Not winter hardy where severe cold is experienced. Needs reasonably fertile soil. |
| Vetch — Hairy | Yes | Widely Adaptable | L | • | Long | 60 | 1½ | ¾ | • | • | • | • | • | Spring<br>Fall | Fall<br>Spring | The most winter hardy vetch. Best sown in fall mixed with winter rye or winter wheat. |
| Vetch — Hungarian | Yes | Heavy Loams | L | | Long | 60 | 1½ | ¾ | • | • | | • | • | Spring<br>Fall | Fall<br>Spring | Next to hairy vetch the most winter hardy of the vetches. Not winter hardy where winters are severe. Needs fairly fertile soil. |
| Vetch — Purple | Yes | Loams | L | | Long | 60 | 1½ | ¾ | • | • | • | • | • | Spring<br>Fall | Fall<br>Spring | Least hardy of the vetches. Suited for winter cover in mild climates only. |
| Vetch — Woolly Pod | Yes | Widely Adaptable | L | | Long | 60 | 1½ | ¾ | • | • | • | • | • | Spring<br>Fall | Fall<br>Spring | |
| Wheat, Winter | No | Loams | L | | Long | 100 | 2½ | ¾ | • | | | • | | Fall | Spring | |

Reprinted from *Improving Garden Soil With Green Manures: A Guide for the Home Gardener*, by Richard Alther and Richard O. Raymond, Garden Way Publishing Co., pp. 22-23.

# III.  ESSENTIAL PLANT NUTRIENTS

Green plants produce their food from simple substances contained in the air and the soil. The most abundant elements in plants are carbon (C), hydrogen (H), and oxygen (O), supplied by carbon dioxide $(CO_2)$ and water $(H_2O)$. The remaining elements essential to plant growth are supplied by the soil. The growth of healthy plants is dependent on a *balance* of these nutrients. Compost, made from a variety of plant materials, manures, and ground rock fertilizers, will maintain the balance of nutrients needed by plants. Green manure crops (legumes) supplement soil nitrogen through the fixation of nitrogen from the plentiful supply in the earth's atmosphere.

Plants need nutrients to build their cells and tissues and to form all the enzymes needed for their vital processes and growth. The essential plant nutrients are commonly divided into those elements needed in relatively large or moderate amounts and those needed in very small or *trace* amounts. There is not a sharp distinction between those needed in moderate or small quantities. The needs of a particular crop determine the amount of each nutrient required for healthy growth. If any one nutrient is deficient (or excessive), a plant will not grow well. A plant nutrient deficiency is indicated through stunted growth and discolored or deformed leaves. However, deficiency symptoms may not appear at all or only during a short period of the growing season. Nutrient deficiency symptoms are often similar, making it difficult to determine which nutrient is lacking. If you maintain the fertility of your soil through additions of compost, it is unlikely that your soil will be deficient in any of the essential plant nutrients.

## MAJOR PLANT NUTRIENTS

*Nitrogen* (N) is essential for the growth of healthy, green, succulent plants. Nitrogen is basic to all living cells, as it is a constituent of proteins and nucleic acids. Nitrogen is also a part of chlorophyll, which imparts the green color to plants and functions in photosynthesis. A deficiency of nitrogen results in stunted growth and pale green or yellow leaves. Older plant leaves become light green, then yellow, and finally brown, as the nitrogen they contain is transferred to the actively growing parts of the plant. An overabundance of nitrogen increases vegetative growth and delays the formation of flowers and fruits. Too much soil nitrogen increases the leaf growth of green pepper plants, inhibiting the formation of fruits. Manure and cottonseed meal are good sources of nitrogen.

*Phosphorus* (P) is an element of plant cells and is essential for cell division and plant growth. Phosphorus is needed for the healthy growth of roots and the development of seeds. A plant deficient in phosphorus tends to have dark or blue-green leaves, with a purple-red discoloration of leaf margins and stems. Phosphate rock and bone meal provide large amounts of phosphorus. Chicken and sheep manure are also rich in this essential nutrient.

*Potassium* (K) is not a constituent of plant tissue, but is important in all plant functions, such as photosynthesis and the formation of fruits and seeds. A deficiency of potassium is indicated by stunted growth and brown, scorched leaves. The leaves may appear yellowish in the areas between the leaf veins and then become dry at the tips and outer margins.  Some leaves, such as those of carrot and tomato, curl up at the leaf margins when there is not enough potassium in the soil.   Wood ashes are the richest source of potassium. Other sources include granite dust, greensand, seaweed, and cottonseed meal.

## SECONDARY NUTRIENTS

*Calcium* (Ca) is an important element of plant cell walls and is an activator for several enzymes.   It is essential for good root growth, and, consequently, healthy plant growth. Sufficient calcium helps to buffer the effects of an unbalanced supply of nutrients and neutralizes acidity in the soil.   A deficiency of calcium results in wrinkled or distorted leaves, often with curled leaf tips and margins.   Ground limestone, dolomite, wood ashes, bone meal, eggshells, and oyster shells are all sources of calcium.

*Magnesium* (Mg) is an essential element of chlorophyll and is needed by all green plants.  It also seems to be important in the transport of phosphorus in the plant.   Magnesium accumulates in the seeds of plants rich in oil, along with an accumulation of lecithin, a fat containing phosphorus.  The addition of magnesium to the soil (rather than phosphorus) may increase the content of phosphorus in a plant.  A lack of magnesium causes plant leaves to lose their green color and drop prematurely.   In many plants, the area between the veins of the leaf turn a reddish purple, while the veins remain green.   Dolomite contributes a large amount of magnesium. Magnesium is contained in green plant materials, sea water, and phosphate rock.  Poultry and sheep manure are high in magnesium.

*Sulfur* (S) is important in the formation of proteins and the development of a good root system. A deficiency of sulfur results in stunted plants and pale green or yellowish leaves, similar to those resulting from nitrogen deficiency. Gypsum and sea water contribute sulfur. Rain carries some sulfur to the soil from air near the sea or near industrial areas, where sulfur-containing fuels are burned.

## TRACE ELEMENTS

Trace elements are needed in very small amounts for normal plant growth. Trace elements are usually parts of enzymes, activating or regulating many reactions taking place in plants, and are not a part of plant tissue. However, too much of a trace element is toxic and potentially more destructive to plants than a deficiency. A trace element deficiency affects the healthy growth of plants and can make them susceptible to disease or insect attack. To be sure that your compost has the necessary trace elements, you can add ground rock fertilizers (like phosphate rock and dolomite).

*Iron* is essential for the formation of chlorophyll and the production of carbohydrates. An iron deficiency causes stunted growth and yellow mottling or striping of plant leaves, particularly those of fruit trees. An excess of lime in the soil can create an iron deficiency. Iron in soil is often in an insoluble form. However, compost (humus) acts as a chelator, making sufficient iron available to the plants. Manure, weeds, seaweed, phosphate rock, and greensand can contribute additional iron to your compost and your soil.

*Manganese* is important in plant enzyme systems. A deficiency, often occurring in overlimed soils, causes stunted growth and yellow mottling of leaves. The unavailability or lack of manganese in soils is responsible for the "grey speck" condition of oats. Manure is a good source of manganese. Seaweed, grass clippings, and phosphate rock are also sources of manganese.

*Copper* is a component of many important plant enzymes, such as those functioning in respiration. In many plants, copper deficiency results in poor chlorophyll formation. Crops such as wheat, barley, and oats will grow strongly on copper-deficient soil, but then will set no seed. A deficiency of copper may be indicated by withered tips of young plant leaves. Sources of copper are sawdust, wood shavings, grass clippings, and phosphate rock.

*Zinc* is important in cell division and seed formation and is a component of several amino acids. Zinc deficiency is fairly widespread in soils around the country. A deficiency of zinc causes distorted and yellow or white spotted leaves. A lack of zinc can result in "apple and peach rosette" in which trees lose many leaves along their branches, but develop whorls of small leaves on their branch tips. Use manure or phosphate rock to prevent zinc deficiency in your soil.

*Boron* is important in cell division and other growth processes. It influences the uptake and utilization of calcium.

Boron deficiency causes the leaves of plant shoot tips to wither and die. In crops such as beets, turnips, cauliflower, and cabbage, a lack of boron results in decayed crowns, distorted leaves, and decayed or hollow roots and stems. Phosphate rock and granite dust are sources of boron. Rainwater near the sea can carry boron to the soil.

*Molybdenum* is a component of various enzymes and is important in nitrogen fixation. The yellowing and infolding of leaf margins are common symptoms of a deficiency of molybdenum, usually a problem only in acid soils. A surplus of molybdenum is generally more of a problem than a shortage, since molybdenum is a pollutant in industrial smoke.

Other trace elements, whose role in plants is not yet clearly understood, may be needed for optimum plant growth. A few of these trace elements are chlorine, sodium, silicon, and aluminum.

# IV.  CARING FOR YOUR TOOLS

"A good tool should last forever." Good tool or bad, the proper care will greatly extend their lives. Be they in the shop, garden or kitchen, the following practices will help keep many of your tools in good shape. In some cases, better than new.

Most people know that tools should be kept clean, dry and out of the rain. But your climate can cause problems even if you hardly ever use the tool. Dry climates cause the wood to dry, shrink and split. Moisture in the air in other climates can be absorbed by the wood causing swelling; then it evaporates, causing drying, and all the while rusting the steel.

So, to keep your tools in prime condition: GIVE EACH TOOL ITS OWN CLEAN, DRY STORAGE PLACE. PUT THE TOOL AWAY CLEAN AND DRY AFTER EACH USE. GIVE THEM INTENSIVE CARE AS NEEDED (at least once a year, and often if they are used hard.)

Clean the metal parts with dry steel wool to remove dirt and rust. For good tool steel use 00 wool (available from most hardware stores), for garden tools a coarser wool is fine. You usually won't need to use water. For a really hard job like getting pitch off saw blades, get some good rubber gloves and a discarded toothbrush. Mix a small amount of lye (one or two tablespoons) into a paste with some water. Be really careful with the lye - the smallest amount can burn you badly. Wear the gloves, and use the toothbrush to apply the lye paste to the sawblade. Brush gently in all the dirty areas to remove the pitch, then rinse carefully but thoroughly to remove every trace of the lye. When the steel is clean and dry on whatever tool, apply a thin film of oil. Good machine oil is fine for saws and such (Japanese carpenters use Camelia oil) and mineral oil is best for any surface that is going to come into contact with food. You want just enough oil on the surface to protect the metal from moisture, not so much that it is greasy.

To care for the wooden parts, you want to sand them first. Use 100 or 120 grit sandpaper for wood in good condition, and 80 grit paper for garden tool handles that are a little weathered. When you have a good clean surface, apply liberally a mixture of:

> 9 parts Linseed Oil
> 1 part Turpentine (synthetic or natural)

The turpentine increases the penetration of the oil, therefore giving more protection. There is no need for a higher percentage - 10% is the optimum. If the wood soaks up the oil, keep applying it until it will stay glossy for a few minutes. Allow the oil to sit for 20 minutes or so, then wipe off any excess. Now you have an oily rag that can easily catch fire-I usually keep mine in a tin can that has a tight fitting lid. The Linseed Oil mixture should be kept in a tightly closed container to prevent evaporation and fires. It can be used on any wooden surface, except those on which you prepare food. Many vegetable oils get rancid in wood, and cabinetmakers recommend mineral oil for food surfaces.

Keep your tools sharp at all times. You can use a coarse file to sharpen shovels and hoes (you will be amazed what a difference it can make to sharpen your garden tools.) For other tools you will need a good stone or two and a book of instruction - keeping tool edges sharp is a whole art in itself.

A good tool kept in good condition is a joy to use and always makes your work incredibly easier. Always use the right tool for the right job, treat your tools gently and respectfully, and they will work better for you, and maybe last forever.

So, to keep your tools in prime condition: Give each tool its own clean, dry storage place. Put the tool away clean and dry after each use. Give them intensive care as needed (at least once a year, and often if they are used hard.)        *LIL LEA*

# V. SOURCES OF SUPPLY

## COMPOST

California Compost Corporation
1601 Skyway Drive—Suite 120
Bakersfield, California 93308

Compost is available in bags, pickup loads, and multiton loads

## EARTHWORMS

North American Bait Farms
1207 South Palmetto
Ontario, California 91761

## SCIENTIFIC SUPPLIES

Capel-Klang
1200 San Mateo Avenue
San Francisco, California 94101

Soil-test kits

Carolina Biological Supply Company
2700 York Road
Burlington, North Carolina 27215

Litmus paper
pH ribbon
Soil-test kits

Fisher Scientific Company
52 Fadem Road
Springfield, New Jersey 07081

Litmus paper
pH ribbon
Soil-test kits

At the time of this writing, Fisher Scientific Company has 21 offices in the United States and 9 in Canada. They ask that you write to the Springfield, New Jersey, office indicating the items in which you are interested. They will then send you catalog pages and the address of the office nearest you.

Reagents, Inc.
P.O. Box 3977
3004 Bank Street
Charlotte, North Carolina 28203

Litmus paper
pH ribbon

Sudbury Laboratories
572 Dutton Road
Sudbury, Massachusetts 01776

Soil-test kits

## COMPOSTING TOILETS

ASI Environment Division
2 Industrial Parkway
Woburn, Massachusetts 01801

Mull-Toa
Soddy Potty #2

Bio-Utility Systems, Inc.
P.O. Box 135
Narberth, Pennsylvania 19072

Mull-Toa

Clivus Multrum USA, Inc.
14A Eliot Street
Cambridge, Massachusetts 02138

Clivus Multrum
Bio Loo

Enviroscope, Inc.
P.O. Box 752
Corona del Mar, California 92625

Toa Throne

Recreation Ecology Conservation of
United States, Inc.
9809 West Bluemound Road
Milwaukee, Wisconsin 53226

Mullbank (Ecolet)

# GLOSSARY

*Ammonium sulfate:* A chemical compound used as an artificial fertilizer, containing 21 percent nitrogen and 24 percent sulfur. Ammonium sulfate is strongly acid in the soil and is deadly to certain beneficial bacteria and earthworms.

*Bone meal:* Bone crushed or ground, usually after extraction of fat and gelatin. Bone meal is used chiefly as a fertilizer, but is used also in the feed of farm animals. Along with phosphate rock, bone meal is the major source of phosphorus for the garden.

*Calcium carbonate:* The major constituent of limestones, dolomite, eggshells, pearls, marbles, chalks, oyster shells, and corals. Calcium carbonate is a white powder that is insoluble in water except in the presence of carbon dioxide.

*Carbohydrates:* Any group of organic compounds composed of carbon, hydrogen, and oxygen. Important carbohydrates include starch and cellulose in plants, glycogen in animals, and sucrose from sugarcane and sugar beets.

*Cellulose:* The main polysaccharide (a complex carbohydrate) in living plants, forming the skeletal structure of the plant cell wall.

*Chelator:* A compound which clamps onto metals and holds them within organic molecules. The grabbing action of chelators makes elements more available to growing plants. Most organic matter has some chelating ability.

*Chlorophyll:* A pigment present in the leaves and stems of green plants. Chlorophyll functions in photosynthesis by absorbing specific wavelengths of sunlight, thus providing the energy for synthesis of carbohydrates.

*Cold frame:* A glass-covered frame used to protect plants and seedlings. The use of a cold frame enables the gardener to start seeds in a protected environment earlier than would otherwise be possible and to accustom seedlings to a more rigorous environment.

*Colloid:* A substance, ordinarily regarded as insoluble, in the form of microscopic particles which remain suspended indefinitely in a suitable medium. Soil colloids are of great importance to the soil. "Colloid" is derived from the Greek word for glue, and refers to the very finely divided, jellylike, residue plant material in the soil. Organic colloidal matter, or humus, increases the water and mineral-holding capacity of the soil.

*Dolomite:* A natural mineral consisting of a calcium magnesium carbonate, found in extensive beds as a compact limestone. Dolomitic limestone is used as a soil amendment.

*Enzyme:* Any of a group of complex organic substances that accelerate or catalyze specific chemical transformations, as in the digestion of foods or organic matter. Without enzymes, microorganisms would not function, and organic matter would remain unchanged.

*Granite dust (Granite stone meal):* An abundant natural source of potash, containing approximately 3 to 5 percent.

*Greensand:* An undersea deposit which contains traces of almost all the elements which occur in sea water. Greensand is a glauconite potash mineral, containing 7 percent of available potash. Greensand absorbs and holds large amounts of water in the soil surface layers and provides an abundant source of plant-available potash. Due to the fact that greensand contains virtually all elements occurring in sea water, its presence in the soil will compensate for existing soil deficiencies.

*Gypsum:* A hydrated calcium sulfate, occurring in extensive beds with other minerals in sedimentary formations. Gypsum also occurs in limestones, dolomite, and some shales. Gypsum is sometimes called sulfate of lime. It helps liberate potash for plant use, but its sulfur content tends to make the soil acid, so its effect is opposite to that of lime.

*Hull:* The outer covering of a fruit or seed.

*Humus:* Finely divided organic matter in soil, derived from microbial decomposition of plant and animal materials. Humus is valued by farmers and gardeners because it provides nutrients essential for plant growth, increases soil water absorption, and improves soil workability.

*Limestone:* A sedimentary rock consisting of more than 95 percent calcium carbonate. Ground limestone is used in soils as an alkalizer to raise the pH factor of the soil and is a source of calcium.

*Lint:* A fibrous coat of thick, convoluted hairs borne by the seeds of cotton plants and contributing the staple of cotton fiber after ginning.

*Litmus paper:* A white or colored (red, blue, or violet) unsized paper, saturated by litmus in water, which is used as a pH indicator. Litmus, obtained from several lichens, is a coloring matter that turns red in acid solutions and blue in alkaline solutions.

*Methane:* A colorless, odorless gas that occurs abundantly in nature as the chief constituent of natural gas. Methane is a product of anaerobic bacterial decomposition of organic materials.

*Photosynthesis:* The process by which chlorophyll-containing cells in green plants convert light to chemical energy and synthesize organic compounds from inorganic compounds—especially carbohydrates from carbon dioxide and water—with the simultaneous release of oxygen.

*Potash:* Any of several compounds containing potassium, especially soluble compounds used chiefly in fertilizers.

*Quicklime (Calcium oxide):* A caustic white solid soluble in water. The commercial form is prepared by roasting calcium carbonate limestone in kilns until all the carbon dioxide is driven off.

*Slaked lime (Hydrate of lime):* Quicklime which has been combined with water. Slaked lime is lime in a readily available condition.

*Windrow:* A method of composting large amounts of material by placing garbage and other wastes in open piles. Windrows may be used in any convenient length, but the depth is somewhat critical. A maximum depth of 5 or 6 feet and a minimum of 4 feet is recommended.

# NOTES

## CHAPTER 1

1. Reprinted from *The Organic Method Primer* ©1973 by Bargyla and Glyver Rateaver, p. 69.
2. Reprinted from *The Complete Book of Composting* ©1960 by J. I. Rodale. Permission granted by Rodale Press, Inc., Emmaus, Pa. 18049, p. 851.

## CHAPTER 2

1. From *How To Grow More Vegetables Than You Ever Thought Possible On Less Land Than You Can Imagine* ©1974, Ecology Action of the Midpeninsula, 2225 El Camino Real, Palo Alto, Calif. 94306, p. 27.

## CHAPTER 4

1. *Organic Method Primer*, Rateaver and Rateaver, p. 67.
2. Ibid., p. 30.
3. Reprinted from *The Encyclopedia of Organic Gardening* ©1959 by J. I. Rodale. Permission granted by Rodale Press, Inc., Emmaus, Pa. 18049, p. 661.
4. Ibid., p. 662.
5. Ibid., p. 843.

## CHAPTER 5

1. *Complete Book of Composting*, Rodale, p. 241.
2. Ibid., pp. 240-1.

## CHAPTER 6

1. Ibid., p. 64.
2. Reprinted from *Composting* ©1972 by Rodale Press, Inc. Permission granted by Rodale Press, Inc., Emmaus, Pa. 18049, p. 87.
3. Ibid., p. 29.
4. Ibid., p. 87.

## CHAPTER 9

1. Reprinted from *The Soil and Health* by Sir Albert Howard © 1947 by the Devin-Adair Company, Inc., Old Greenwich, Conn. 06870. Permission granted by the publisher, p. 38.
2. Ibid., p. 38.

## CHAPTER 10

1. From *Growing Your Own Mushrooms: Cultivating, Cooking and Preserving*, by Jo Mueller. Permission granted by Garden Way Publishing Co., p. 23.
2. Ibid., p. 24.
3. Ibid., pp. 12, 22.

## CHAPTER 11

1. *Complete Book of Composting*, Rodale, pp. 314-315.

## CHAPTER 12

1. From *Down-to-Earth Vegetable Gardening Know-How*, by Dick Raymond. Permission granted by Garden Way Publishing Co., p. 83.
2. *Organic Method Primer*, Rateaver and Rateaver, p. 89.
3. Ibid., p. 79.
4. *How to Grow More Vegetables*, Ecology Action, p. 26.

## CHAPTER 14

1. Reprinted from *The Basic Book of Organic Gardening*, © 1971 by Rodale Press, Inc. Permission granted by Rodale Press, Inc., Emmaus, Pa. 18049, pp. 57-58.

## CHAPTER 15

1. From *Earthworms for Ecology and Profit*, Volume II © 1977 by Ronald E. Gaddie, Sr. and Donald E. Douglas. Reprinted by permission of publisher, Bookworm Publishing Co., p. 127.
2. *Composting: A Review of Rationale, Principles and Public Health*, by C. G. Golueke. *Compost Science* 17 (1976): 11-15. Published by Rodale Press, Inc., Emmaus, Pa. 18049.
3. Reprinted from *Garbage As You Like It* © 1969 by Rodale Books, Inc. Permission granted by Rodale Press, Inc., Emmaus, Pa. 18049.
4. Ibid.
5. *Composting Sewage Sludge: How?* by G. B. Wilson and J. M. Walker. *Compost Science* 14 (1973): 30-32. Published by Rodale Press, Inc., Emmaus, Pa. 18049.

# BIBLIOGRAPHY

Alther, Richard, and Raymond, Richard O. *Improving Garden Soil with Green Manures: A Guide for the Home Gardener*. Charlotte, Vermont: Garden Way Publishing Co., 1974.

Campbell, Stu. *The Mulch Book*. Charlotte, Vermont: Garden Way Publishing Co., 1973.

Darwin, Charles. *The Formation of Vegetable Mould through the Action of Worms*. New York: D. Appleton and Co., 1898.

Gaddie, Sr., Ronald E., and Douglas, Donald E. *Earthworms for Ecology & Profit*. Vol. I and Vol. II. Ontario, California: Bookworm Publishing Co., 1977.

Goldstein, J. *Garbage As You Like It: A Plan to Stop Pollution by Using Our Nation's Wastes*. Emmaus, Pennsylvania: Rodale Press, 1969.

Golueke, Clarence G. *Composting: A Study of the Process and its Principles*. Emmaus, Pennsylvania: Rodale Press, 1972.

——. "Composting: A Review of Rationale, Principles and Public Health." *Compost Science* 17 (1976): 11-15.

Gotaas, H. B. *Composting: Sanitary Disposal and Reclamation of Organic Wastes*. Geneva, Switzerland: World Health Organization, 1956.

Harris, Bob. *Growing Wild Mushrooms: A Complete Guide to Cultivating Edible and Hallucinogenic Mushrooms*. Berkeley, California: Wingbow Press, 1976.

Howard, Sir Albert. *The Soil and Health: A Study of Organic Agriculture*. New York: Schocken Books, 1947.

Jeavons, John. *How to Grow More Vegetables Than You Ever Thought Possible on Less Land Than You Can Imagine*. Palo Alto, California: Ecology Action of the Midpeninsula, 1974.

Koepf, H. H. *Compost: What It Is—How It Is Made—What It Does*. Stroudsburg, Pennsylvania: Bio-Dynamic Farming and Gardening Association, Inc., 1966.

Logsdon, Gene. *The Gardener's Guide to Better Soil*. Emmaus, Pennsylvania: Rodale Press, 1975.

Martin, J., Leonard, W., and Stamp, D. *Principles of Field Crop Production*. New York: Macmillan Publishing Co., Inc., 1976.

Mueller, Jo. *Growing Your Own Mushrooms: Cultivating, Cooking and Preserving*. Charlotte, Vermont: Garden Way Publishing Co., 1976.

Pfeiffer, E. E. *The Art and Science of Composting*. Stroudsburg, Pennsylvania: Bio-Dynamic Farming and Gardening Association, Inc., 1959.

Rateaver, Bargyla, and Rateaver, Glyver. *The Organic Method Primer*. Pauma Valley, California: By the authors, 1973.

Raymond, Dick. *Down-to-Earth Vegetable Gardening Know-How*. Charlotte, Vermont: Garden Way Publishing Co., 1975.

Rodale, J. I. *The Encyclopedia of Organic Gardening.* Emmaus, Pennsylvania: Rodale Press, 1959.

——. *The Complete Book of Composting.* Emmaus, Pennsylvania: Rodale Press, 1960.

——. *How to Grow Fruits and Vegetables by the Organic Method.* Emmaus, Pennsylvania: Rodale Press, 1961.

Rodale, Robert. *The Basic Book of Organic Gardening.* New York: Ballantine Books, 1971.

Russell, E. W. *Soil Conditions and Plant Growth.* London and New York: Longman, 1973.

Savage, J., Chase, T., and Macmillan, J. D. "Population Changes in Enteric Bacteria and Other Microorganisms during Aerobic Thermophilic Windrow Composting." *Applied Microbiology* 26 (1973): 969-974.

Willson, G. B., and Walker, J. M. "Composting Sewage Sludge: How?" *Compost Science* 14 (1973): 30-32.

# INDEX

# EASY REFERENCE GUIDE FOR
# BUILDING YOUR COMPOST HEAP

## Compost Materials

Branches (an armful or two)
Wooden poles (3 or 4)
Hay
Grass clippings
Leaves
Weeds
Sawdust
Kitchen garbage
Manure (horse, cow, dog, chicken, rabbit)
Wood ash or limestone
Rich topsoil
Water

## Getting It All Together

1. Loosen the soil which will be underneath the compost heap. An area at least 3 feet square is a good size to begin with.

2. Push 3 or 4 wooden poles into the loosened soil until they stand up easily. Space the poles evenly in the area the compost heap will cover. These will make vertical aeration holes in the compost heap.

3. Lay down a latticework of branches over the soil. This provides some air circulation underneath the compost heap.

4. Cover the layer of branches with a 5- to 6-inch layer of hay, leaves, or other plant materials. If you use many different materials, your compost will contain a wide variety of nutrients.

5. Spread a layer of kitchen waste, which has been accumulated in a tight-lidded container.

6. Cover the layer of plant materials and kitchen waste with a 2-inch layer of manure to provide an adequate supply of nitrogen.

7. Spread a *thin* layer (about 1/8 inch) of rich topsoil mixed with a light sprinkling of wood ash or limestone.

8. Moisten the layers thoroughly, if needed, until the materials feel as moist as a damp sponge or towel which has been wrung out. Moisten the compost heap as you build it. Be careful not to saturate the heap.

9. Continue layering the compost materials until the heap is 3 to 5 feet high. Combine different textures and alternate wet and dry materials, like green grass clippings and hay.

10. Cover the finished compost heap with a layer of soil and a thick layer of hay for insulation.

11. Lightly press the top of the compost heap to form a shallow basin to catch rainfall. In an area with heavy rainfall leave the heap rounded on top. Water the compost heap with a hose when there is not enough rainfall.

*Note:* More detailed instructions for building your compost heap can be found in chapter 9.

# EASY REFERENCE GUIDE FOR
# BUILDING A SIMPLE WOODEN BIN

## *Materials*

Wood
    Frame:  2 pieces, 2 by 2 by 36 inches
             2 pieces, 2 by 2 by 38 inches
    Sides:   32 pieces, 1 by 4 by 36 inches
    Furring strips:  2 pieces, 1 by 3 by 36 inches
    Roof:   1 piece, 40-inch square
            (or half an old door)
            (or corrugated tin)

*Caution:* Actual wood sizes are smaller than the dimensions given. When you ask for a 1- by 4-inch piece of wood, the actual size is 3/4- by 3 1/2-inch.

Hardware
    # 3 galvanized nails (1 1/4-inch)
    # 6 galvanized nails (2-inch)
    4 medium-sized hasps (2 1/2-inch)

## *Instructions*

1. Place the 38-inch frame posts toward the front side of the bin and the 36-inch frame posts toward the rear.

2. Nail the side slats to the frame posts, leaving 1-inch spaces between slats. (The front frame posts must be 3/4 -inch from the end of the slats to allow sufficient space for the furring strips which hold the front gate together. The front gate must lie flat against the rest of the frame.)

3. Nail the rear slats to the 36-inch frame posts to complete 3 sides of the bin.

4. Nail the front slats to the furring strips and attach the 4 hasps to hold the front gate to the frame.

5. Set the roof over the bin frame. The roof slants toward the rear of the bin to direct heavy rain run-off. The roof can be removed and replaced to regulate watering, catching rainfall as needed.

   *Note:* If you want to treat the wood of your bin to preserve it longer, use linseed oil. Creosote should not be used on compost bins, because it is a toxic substance which can hinder the growth of microorganisms and plants.

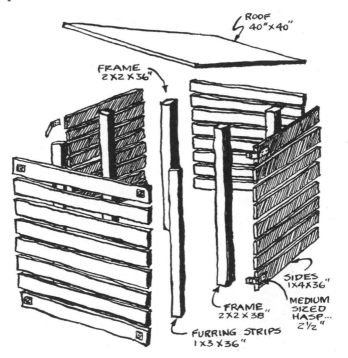

A wooden bin with finished dimensions of 3 by 3 by 3 feet can be constructed with readily available materials.